Improve your Skills

Listening & Speaking for IELTS
with Answer Key
4.5–6.0

Barry Cusack • Sam McCarter

MACMILLAN

Macmillan Education
4 Crinan Street
London N1 9XW
A division of Macmillan Publishers Limited

Companies and representatives throughout the world

ISBN 978-0-230-46468-1 (with key + Audio Pack)
ISBN 978-0-230-46467-4 (without key + Audio Pack)
ISBN 978-0-230-46287-8 (with key + MPO Pack)
ISBN 978-0-230-46286-1 (without key + MPO Pack)

Text, design and illustration © Macmillan Publishers Limited 2014

Written by Barry Cusack and Sam McCarter

The authors have asserted their rights to be identified as the authors of this work in accordance with the Copyright, Designs and Patents Act 1988.

First published 2014

All rights reserved; no part of this publication may be reproduced, stored in a retrieval system, transmitted in any form, or by any means, electronic, mechanical, photocopying, recording, or otherwise, without the prior written permission of the publishers.

Designed by Kamae Design, Oxford
Cover design by Macmillan
Cover photograph by Digital Vision
Picture research by Susannah Jayes

Barry Cusack and Sam McCarter would like to thank the editors.

The publishers would like to thanks all those who participated in the development of the project, with special thanks to the freelance editors.

The authors and publishers would like to thank the following for permission to reproduce their photographs:
Alamy/aberCPC p30, Alamy/Arcaid Images p6(cm), Alamy/A.Astes p6(cl), Alamy/BUILT Images p6(bcl), Alamy/ F1online digitale Bildagentur GmbH p47, Alamy/Emmanuel Lacoste p65, Alamy/moodboard p34, Alamy/Jeff Morgan 03 p31, Alamy/Alan Novelli p62, Alamy/Paul Thompson p78, Alamy/Paris Eiffel Tower p43; Corbis/Thomas van Bracht/Demotix p70(tc), **Corbis**/Neil Guegan/Image Source p80, Corbis/John Kraus/moodboard p11, Corbis/RelaXimages p48; **DIGITAL VISION** p54(cl); Getty Images/RYO/a.collectionRF p39, Getty Images/Paul Bradbury p72, Getty Images/Gustav Klimt/Bridgeman p58, **Getty Images**/Danita Delimont p83, Getty Images/Fuse p42, Getty Images/UIG via Getty Images p46, Getty Images/GUIZIOU Franck/hemis.fr p70(cl), Getty Images/Justin Hutchinson p23(cr), Getty Images/Tomaz Levstek p26, Getty Images/Popperfoto p57, Getty Images/Paul Thompson p51; **Image Source** p23(bcr); Macmillan Australia p67; Photodisc p84, Photodisc/Getty Images p32; **Photoshot**/TTL p64; **Press Association Images** p38; Superstock/Stockbroker p54(tl), **Superstock**/Westend61 p74; **Thinkstock**/Istockphoto pp15,70(tr).

Although we have tried to trace and contact copyright holders before publication, in some cases this has not been possible. If contacted we will be pleased to rectify any errors or omissions at the earliest opportunity.

Printed and bound in Thailand

2018 2017 2016 2015 2014
10 9 8 7 6 5 4 3 2 1

Contents

Introduction
page 4

	Topic	Listening skills	Speaking skills
Unit 1 page 6	Change and consequences	Predicting in tables	Identifying yourself Discussing familiar topics Saying where you come from Pronunciation: stressing syllables
Unit 2 page 14	The importance of the past	Understanding signpost phrases Answering sentence completion questions Answering matching questions	Describing a past event Informal speech: using signpost phrases Planning your talk in Part 2 Describing precautions Pronunciation: linking in connected speech
Unit 3 page 22	Machines, cycles and processes	Understanding information in flow charts	Answering Part 3 questions Introducing opinions Pronunciation: using opinion phrases
Unit 4 page 30	Education	Identifying campus contexts Using information in multiple-choice questions Answering summary completion questions	Describing people Making notes Pronunciation: placing stress in compound nouns
Unit 5 page 38	Youth	Understanding maps Answering sentence and table completion questions	Describing jobs Stating advantages and disadvantages Pronunciation: stressing compound adjectives
Unit 6 page 46	Culture	Understanding layout Understanding noun phrases Predicting from notes	Talking about free time activities Expressing preferences Dealing with unfamiliar topics Pronunciation: shifting syllable stress
Unit 7 page 54	Arts and sciences	Making questions from statements Paraphrasing for matching	Comparing and evaluating Expressing others' views Pronunciation: weak forms and /ə/
Unit 8 page 62	Nature	Changing opinions Answering multiple-choice questions Completing a summary (2)	Describing animals Describing presents Pronunciation: contrastive stress
Unit 9 page 70	Health	Predicting in tables (2) Spelling words	Recognizing similar questions Emphasizing main points Taking time to think Pronunciation: using two intonation patterns
Unit 10 page 78	The individual and society	Paraphrasing questions Answering visual multiple-choice questions	Describing places and feelings Starting your description Summing up impressions Pronunciation: using intonation in continuous speech

Phonemic Chart
page 86

Answer Key
page 87

Introduction

What is *Improve your IELTS Listening and Speaking Skills*?

Improve your IELTS Listening and Speaking Skills is a complete preparation course for students at score bands 4.5–6.00 preparing for the Listening and Speaking components of the International English Language Testing System. Through targeted practice, it develops skills and language to help you achieve a higher IELTS score in these two components.

How can I use this book?

You can use *Improve your IELTS Listening and Speaking Skills* as a book for studying on your own or in a class.

If you are studying on your own, *Improve Your IELTS Listening and Speaking Skills* is designed to guide you step by step through the activities. The book is completely self-contained: a clear and accessible key is provided, so you can easily check your answers as you work through the book. There are two CDs which contain all the recorded material necessary for the Listening skills and Speaking skills sections of each unit.

If you are studying as part of a class, your teacher will direct you on how to use each activity. Some activities, especially in the Topic talk and Speaking skills sections, provide the opportunity for speaking and discussion practice.

How is *Improve your IELTS Listening and Speaking Skills* organized?

It consists of ten units based around topics which occur commonly in the real test. Each unit consists of:

Topic talk: exercises and activities to introduce vocabulary and ideas useful for the topic.

Listening skills: exercises and activities to develop the skills for questions in the Listening component.

Speaking skills: exercises and activities to develop skills and language for the Speaking component, including practice questions from one part of the module.

Pronunciation focus: exercises and activities to practise key aspects of pronunciation in English.

Exam listening: one complete section of the Listening exam to practise the skills learned.

In addition, there are Techniques boxes throughout the book. These reinforce key points on how to approach Listening and Speaking tasks.

How will *Improve your IELTS Listening and Speaking Skills* improve my score?

By developing skills

The skills sections of each unit form a detailed syllabus of essential IELTS Listening and Speaking skills. For example, in Listening skills there is coverage of *Signpost phrases* and *Prediction skills*. In Speaking skills, there is coverage of *Comparing and evaluating* as well as *Describing advantages and disadvantages*. There is also Pronunciation practice at the end of the Speaking skills sections.

By developing language

The Topic talk part of each unit develops vocabulary, phrases and sentence forms for use in the Listening and Speaking components. The Speaking skills section has phrases to help you introduce and organize your spoken answers.

By developing test technique

The Listening skills sections introduce you to the skills you need to tackle the various types of question that can be asked. Knowing the best way to tackle each type of question will enable you to get the best mark you can. The Speaking skills section will make you familiar with the different question types and enable you to relax in the exam and perform at your best.

How is the IELTS Listening component organized?

It consists of four sections: usually there are two monologues and two conversations on a variety of topics. There are ten questions in each section. The topics cover everyday social matters and subjects related to educational or training situations. You hear the recording only once, but you have time to look at the questions first and further time to write your answers.

What kind of questions are there?

There are a variety of question types including multiple-choice, matching, short answer questions, sentence completion, form/table completion, labelling a diagram/plan/map, classification of information, matching information and summary.

How will I be assessed?

You will get one mark for each correct answer up to a maximum of 40 marks. The questions gradually increase in difficulty, but all the marks have the same value.

How is the IELTS Speaking component organized?

You have a one-to-one interview with an examiner lasting between eleven and fourteen minutes. There are three parts. Firstly, the examiner asks questions on everyday topics such as family, hobbies and likes and dislikes. Secondly, you speak for one to two minutes on a topic given by the examiner. Finally, you take part in a discussion on more abstract issues linked to the topic of the talk.

How will I be assessed?

The examiner awards marks under four headings:

Fluency and coherence: speaking in a continuous way, without unnatural hesitation, and organizing your thoughts and speech in a logical way.

Lexical resource: using a range of vocabulary appropriate to the topic.

Grammatical range and accuracy: using a range of grammatical forms, including more complex forms, with a reasonable degree of accuracy.

Pronunciation: speaking so that you can be understood by the examiner.

1 Change and consequences

UNIT AIMS

LISTENING SKILLS
Predicting in tables

SPEAKING SKILLS
Identifying yourself
Discussing familiar topics
Saying where you come from
Pronunciation: stressing syllables

Topic talk

1 Look at the advertisements and answer the questions below.
  a Is rented accommodation expensive where you live? Why/Why not?
  b How can students be helped with accommodation when they move away from home?
  c Which accommodation would you apply for, a or b? Why?

2 Make a list of types of accommodation that you know.

3 Write your own advertisement (15–20 words). This can be based on your own accommodation.

4 Complete sentences a–g with the words in the list.
  Example
  Here in Australia, I live in a large ___*flat*___ in a twenty-storey tower block.

a Room available in large, central apartment in return for looking after pets and general duties. Must be reliable, tidy and a non-smoker. Would suit female student.

b Studio available. £700 a month, excluding bills. Twenty minutes by train from London. Single occupant only.

| shared house ■ studio ■ farmhouse ■ house ■ flat ■ bungalow ■ penthouse terraced house |

  a I'd love to live in a _____ on the top floor of a tower block.
  b In my home country, I live in the capital in a spacious detached _____.
  c I can't afford to live in a large flat so I am renting a small _____.
  d My parents live in a remote two-storey _____ on a mountainside.
  e As my grandmother can't climb stairs and hates lifts, she lives in a _____ in the suburbs.
  f My host family live in a red-brick _____ right in the middle of a long row.
  g There are six of us living together in a _____ in a student area of town.

6

Change and consequences

5 Add extra information to four of the sentences in exercise 4 using phrases 1–4 below.
1. with spectacular views of the city, especially at night.
2. with lots of open fields around them and plenty of fresh air.
3. which has a kitchen, bedroom and living room all in one. It suits me fine.
4. which can get a bit noisy if all our friends are around.

> **Technique**
> Add information to statements using *with* or *which*. The additional information doesn't need to be long.

6 Decide which adjective in a–g below is the opposite of the other two.
a boring dull fascinating
b cramped spacious sizeable
c traditional modern old-fashioned
d bustling quiet peaceful
e cosy uncomfortable inviting
f smart elegant shabby
g vibrant boring lively

> **Technique**
> Keep a list of new adjectives by theme with examples if possible.

7 Which type of accommodation do you live in? Make a list of adjectives to describe where you live.

8 The questions below come from an IELTS Speaking test. Match the examiner's questions with the candidate's answers.
1. Where do your host family live?
2. How close to the city is it?
3. Is your accommodation modern or old-fashioned?
4. Can you tell me what the area you live in is like?
5. What is your family home like?

a The neighbourhood where I live is very peaceful.
b My parents' apartment is in a very dynamic part of the city,
c The family I'm staying with live in a very chic part of town.
d The house is very high tech,
e It is in a very good location,

9 Develop the sentences a–e in exercise 8 by adding one of the following sentences.
1. because it is well connected to the city centre by train and bus.
2. so it is always noisy and full of people.
3. with plasma screens, remote controls for the lighting and wireless computers.
4. The area is residential with tree-lined streets, no shops and not many cars.
5. At all times of the day it is really tranquil. I have to say I love it there.

10 Which items in exercise 9 give these extra types of information?

Reason _____

Consequence _____

11 Ask and answer the questions in exercise 8.

7

Unit 1

Listening skills Predicting in tables

1 Choose the best title a–c for each table 1–3.
  a Climate change over 50 years
  b Transport use by type
  c Comparison of housing by area

2 Complete each table with the information below.

1

District	Typical style	Average price	Transport
Aberton	bungalows	£180,000	1 _____
Hunborough	2 _____	£225,000	poor
Millview	flats	3 _____	excellent

2

	1955	2013
Average temperature	17.4°C	4 _____
Annual rainfall	5 _____	652 mm

3

	Bus	Train	Bicycle
Price of fare	£1.50	7 _____	N/A
Total journeys	6 _____	2504	962
Male passengers	34%	62%	8 _____
Female passengers	66%	38%	9 _____

£125,000 ■ £4.50 ■ 18.2°C ■ 25% ■ 3567 ■ 612 mm ■ 75% ■ good ■ terraced houses

3 Look at the numbering in the tables. Which tables are read from top to bottom? Which are read from left to right?

Technique

Familiarize yourself with charts and tables. Find them in newspapers and magazines and online, e.g. at www.ons.gov.uk. Learn to read and understand them.

Change and consequences

4 The table below is taken from a table completion task. Read the table contents then answer questions a–d.

	Price now	Main advantage	Second advantage	Length of guarantee	Main disadvantage
Analogue radio	Example: £29.99	Cheap	Excellent 3 _sound quality_ with expensive systems	4 _1 year_	Service will finish soon
Digital radio	1 £ _95_	2 Lots of _stations_	Little or no interference	2 years	5 _Battery life_ is short

→ clarity
→ number and variety

a What is the topic of the table?
b How many products are discussed?
c How many aspects of each product are considered?
d Which answers may be numbers?

5 The instructions for the table completion task in exercise 4 are:
'Write NO MORE THAN TWO WORDS AND/OR A NUMBER for each answer.'
Which of the following answers must be wrong, and why?

a very high quality
b 210
c £35 or £55
d 3 or 4 years

6 🔊 1.1 Listen to the recording, follow the instructions as given in exercise 5 and complete the gaps in the table in exercise 4.

7 The table below is also taken from a table completion task. Read through the table carefully and answer these questions.

a In which order will you hear the information?
b Which answers can you predict?

Technique
Pay special attention to the rubric, the headings and the numbering in table completion tasks. Use this information to predict the type of information which is missing.

	old ValueCard	new SuperValue Card
Points	Standard number	Double points
Free credit period	One month	6 _3_ months
Interest rate	18.5%	7 _22.5_ %
Cardholder shopping evenings	8 _1_ per month	Two per month
Benefits	Free delivery within 9 _20_ miles	Free delivery within 50 miles
Fee	Nil	10 £ _12_

8 🔊 1.2 Listen to the recording and complete the gaps in the table. Write NO MORE THAN ONE WORD AND/OR A NUMBER for each answer.

9

Unit 1

Speaking skills Identifying yourself

Technique
Speak slowly and clearly. In the opening exchange, sound interested in order to make a good first impression.

1 🔊 1.3 Listen to four questions from the start of the IELTS Speaking test. Write the exact questions the examiner asks.

a Can you _____ ?
b And what _____ ?
c Where _____ ?
d Could you _____ ?

2 Read this information about a candidate for the Speaking test. Use the information to complete the dialogue with the examiner.

> Benjamin Weiss is going to take the Speaking module at 3.30 this afternoon. He comes from Switzerland and prefers people to call him Ben. He has brought his passport as identification.

Candidate: Hello, good _____ .
Examiner: Good _____ . Can you _____ me your _____ name, please?
Candidate: My name is _____ .
Examiner: And what can I _____ you?
Candidate: Please _____ me _____ .
Examiner: Good. Where _____ you come _____ ?
Candidate: I come _____ .
Examiner: Can you _____ me your identification, please?
Candidate: Of course. _____ is my _____ .

3 With a partner, practise reading the dialogue above. Then practise again giving answers as yourself.

Discussing familiar topics

1 The following questions are taken from an interview in a daily newspaper with a famous singer. Match the questions 1–8 with her answers a–h.

1 What kind of town did you grow up in?
2 Where would you like to live?
3 Do you have any hobbies?
4 What sort of TV programmes do you like watching?
5 What is your greatest fear?
6 Which living person do you most admire?
7 What is your most precious object?
8 What sort of place do you live in now?

Change and consequences

a I've got this beautiful ring that belonged to my grandmother. It has sentimental value for me. It's very special.
b Spiders.
c In New York, of course.
d I'm quite keen on comedies. I don't particularly like news and current affairs. They make me feel sad.
e Hotels mostly.
f I grew up in quite a small town. It was quiet and nice, and everyone seemed to know everyone else.
g I like playing jazz piano. I like it because it relaxes me.
h My dad. He has taught me such a lot about how to live my life well, and I'm grateful for that.

2 Look again at the questions and answers in exercise 1. Answer the questions below.
   a Are the questions complex and abstract or do they relate to personal information?
   b Which answers would be good in the Speaking test? Why?

3 Make 10 typical questions that examiners ask in Part 1 of the Speaking module. Use the words given to make the full questions, add in extra words such as articles where necessary. The first one has been done for you.

a How often / you / listen / music?
   How often do you listen to music?

b Where / was / last / place / you / travelled / to?

c What form / transport / you / use most?

d When / you / start / learning English?

e Which form / communication / you / like / use / most – / email / phone?

f What sports / you / played?

g What kind / food / like / eat?

h What hobbies / you / have?

i What sort / television programmes / you / enjoy / watching?

j What type / books / you / enjoy / reading?

4 With a partner, ask and answer the questions you wrote in exercise 3. Give extra information to elaborate your answers.

Technique
Prepare for Speaking Part 1 by thinking about the kinds of topic the examiner may ask you about. Prepare also by thinking of extra details to support your answers.

Unit 1

Saying where you come from

1 🔊 1.4 In Speaking Part 1, you will often be asked about your home town or where you live now. Listen to an extract from an interview. Complete the examiner's questions in the spaces below.

> *Now in this first part I'd like to ask you some questions about yourself. Let's talk about your town or village.*
> Question 1: Could you tell me .... ?
> Question 2: What .... ?
> Question 3: Is there anything .... ?
> Question 4: And what kind .... ?

2 🔊 1.4 Listen again. Make notes on the details that the student mentions in response to each question.

Question 1 _____

Question 2 _____

Question 3 _____

Question 4 _____

How much detail does the student give in each answer?

3 Make a note of your own personal answers in response to the questions in exercise 1.

4 With a partner, ask and answer the questions in exercise 1. Try to add extra information to your answers. Use the phrases in the list below to help you.

I used to live in … but now I …
I moved here …
It's a … place with …
What I like about it is … because …
The great thing about … is …
I suppose most people …

> **Technique**
> Always support your answer by adding extra information. Use *for example* and *because*.

Pronunciation: stressing syllables

1 How many syllables are there in each of these words for describing places?

| pleasant ▪ dynamic ▪ flat ▪ peaceful ▪ cramped ▪ bungalow ▪ detached ▪ overpriced |

2 🔊 1.5 Listen to the words and match each word with a stress pattern below.

Example
pleasant   *pattern 2*

Pattern 1 O   Pattern 2 Oo   Pattern 3 oO   Pattern 4 Ooo   Pattern 5 oOo   Pattern 6 ooO

3 Identify which word has a different stress pattern from the rest of the words.

a	discuss	also	although	reply
b	interest	hotel	prefer	technique
c	quality	radio	comedy	solution
d	example	experience	advantage	afternoon
e	technology	variety	information	environment
f	interference	explanation	analysis	sentimental
g	unacceptable	theoretical	unobtainable	communicable

12

Change and consequences

Exam listening

Section 2

🔊 1.6

Questions 11–15

Write **NO MORE THAN THREE WORDS** for each answer.

What three kinds of people are listening to the talk?

11 ....
12 ....
13 ....
14 What will you need to do to visit the Fieldhouse Library?

....

15 What is necessary for gaining access to the library?

....

Technique
Read the questions first to predict what the listening is about. Listen carefully as you will only hear the recording once.

🔊 1.7

Questions 16–20

Write **NO MORE THAN TWO WORDS AND/OR A NUMBER** for each answer.

What are the two collections which have not yet been fully moved in?

16 ....
17 ....
18 What is currently being built?

....

19 How many computer places have been installed?

....

20 What else can you get from the librarians if you ask?

....

Technique
Check the instructions. How many words and/or numbers must you write?

2 The importance of the past

UNIT AIMS

LISTENING SKILLS	SPEAKING SKILLS
Understanding signpost phrases	Describing a past event
Answering sentence completion questions	Informal speech: using signpost phrases
Answering matching questions	Planning your talk in Part 2
	Describing precautions
	Pronunciation: linking in connected speech

Topic talk

1 Look at the pictures with a partner and answer the questions which follow.
   a What do you think each item reminds the speaker of?
   b Does the train ticket trigger happy or sad memories? How do you know?
   c Is there anything which triggers happy memories for you? If so, what?
   d Are your happy memories similar to your partner's?

That was an unforgettable journey…

2 In the phrases below, decide which two adjectives are connected with positive memory.

Example
good unforgettable ceremonial moment

   a suitable marvellous great time
   b happy tragic remarkable event
   c great momentous formal occasion
   d fleeting memorable favourable moment
   e exhilarating rewarding past experience
   f exciting big foreign adventure
   g outstanding minor impressive achievement
   h former golden happy days
   i fantastic business great trip

> **Technique**
> Keep a list of adjectives to describe events from your personal history in the IELTS Speaking Part 2.

The importance of the past

3 Which words from the lists in exercise 2 combine with the words below?
Complete the lists. The first one has been done for you.
thoroughly *exciting*, …
highly …
very …
totally …

4 Match each event a–e with the noun which best describes it.

an achievement
a special occasion
an adventure
an experience
an event

  a studying abroad
  b doing well in exams
  c a musical concert
  d your brother's wedding
  e getting lost

5 For each noun in the list, think of at least one personal experience.
Example
an achievement: *I won a school sports prize.*

6 With a partner, ask and answer questions about the events you noted in exercise 5. Use these prompts to help you.

Tell me about …
What kind of …?
What happened …?

> **Technique**
>
> Use nouns like those in exercise 4 to help trigger ideas in the IELTS Speaking Part 2. Make a list on cards of events, people, places and possessions/items that you are familiar with. Think of how to describe them and give reasons for liking, disliking and remembering them. You might also be asked about events and experiences that were new or exciting.

7 Use nouns to summarize descriptions. Match each event a–h with the descriptions below.

Example
I had a party for my twenty-first birthday. *It was a happy event.*

  a I volunteered to help other young people.
  b I received first prize for a painting I did in secondary school.
  c I want to describe something strange which actually happened in my home town.
  d The journey by coach and train around South America brings back lots of good memories.
  e I attended the inaugural speech of the President.
  f I got lost with some friends in the Australian desert.
  g I parachuted from a plane to celebrate passing my exams.
  h I saw the hardship of other people when I was volunteering.

exhilarating experience
unforgettable moment
formal occasion
rewarding experience
nerve-racking adventure
bizarre incident
humbling experience
memorable trip

8 Make three statements of your own about experiences, events or occasions. Work in pairs and explain your statements to your partner.

Unit 2

Listening skills Understanding signpost phrases

1 The sentences below come from a lecture on history. Decide the function of the phrases in italics in sentences a–i and add them to the list. Note that some sentences may be used more than once.

Starting: _e_

Listing: _____

Adding: _____

Digressing: _____

Returning to the subject: _____

Concluding: _____

a *In addition*, we can ask if the study of history has any practical use.
b *Anyway*, there is a wide range of topics for you to choose from.
c *Finally*, I wish you good luck.
d *By the way*, there is a series of lectures on this topic starting on Tuesday.
e *I'd like to begin* this term's lectures with a few general questions.
f *Secondly*, what is history?
g *To sum up*, as I said, you are fortunate.
h *Firstly*, why study history?
i *Again*, we can look at the different kinds of history there are to study.

2 The sentences below are part of another lecture on a similar topic. Put them in the correct order.

a By the way, there's a lecture on citizenship in the Social Sciences building on Wednesday.
b I'd like to begin by giving three reasons for studying history.
c Finally, we can do better in our jobs if we know a little history.
d Secondly, it helps us to be better citizens: we can participate better in our society if we understand its history.
e Firstly, it helps us to understand the world we live in, especially its politics and economics.
f To sum up, history can be a huge help in many aspects of our lives.
g Anyway, our participation in society is more meaningful if we understand a bit more.

> **Technique**
> Pay attention to linking phrases used in talks and lectures to follow the flow and structure of the recording in Listening Section 4.

Answering sentence completion questions

1 Statements a–f give some facts about sentence completion tasks. Decide whether the statements are true or false.

a You must always put words in the gaps.
b The instructions tell you how many words you need.
c Sometimes you can put a number in the gap.
d The missing information is usually at the start of the sentence.
e Gaps are located at the middle or end of the sentence.
f It is possible to guess what type of information is missing.

The importance of the past

2 The instructions and sentences below are taken from a sentence completion task. Read them carefully and check your answers to exercise 1.

Complete the sentences below. Write **ONE WORD OR A NUMBER** *for each answer.*

The handout covers **1** .... general topics.

As well as students of history, there are students of **2** .... at the lecture.

The lecturer's own motivation for studying history is that she finds it **3** ....

3 🔊 1.8 Listen to the first part of the recording and answer the questions in exercise 2.

Answering matching questions

1 The inventions in the list come from different periods in history. Decide which period A–C they belong to.

A the eighteenth century
B the nineteenth century
C the twentieth century

1 the telephone
2 the automobile
3 the steam engine
4 the aeroplane
5 the typewriter
6 the wristwatch

2 The questions below are taken from a matching task. Can you predict any of the answers?

How does the lecturer describe each kind of history?

T *a traditional type of history*
M *a modern type of history*
F *a type of history which looks to the future*

Write the correct letter **T, M** *or* **F** *next to questions 4–10.*

4 political history ....
5 post-modern history ....
6 feminist history ....
7 social history ....
8 economic history ....
9 military history ....
10 ethnic history ....

3 In the recording you may not hear the exact words *traditional, modern, which looks to the future.* Put the following synonyms in the best place in the table. One has been done for you.

progressive ■ present-day ■ old-fashioned ■ orthodox ■ visionary ■ contemporary
classical ■ up-to-date ■ forward-looking ■ new ■ current ■ conventional

Words in the question	Possible words in the recording
traditional	
modern	
looks to the future	*visionary*

Technique
Read the question carefully in matching tasks. If the categories are related, decide what kinds of words and phrases you would expect to hear. Listen for similar information in the recording.

4 🔊 1.9 Listen to the second part of the recording and answer the questions in exercise 2.

17

Unit 2

Speaking skills Describing a past event

1 Read these two advertisements and answer questions a–d.
   a Where would you see advertisements like these?
   b Do you think the owner will find her purse? What about the owner of the wallet?
   c What do you think about the reward? Is it large enough, or too large?
   d What would you do if you lost a wallet or a purse?

FOUND
Lady's purse. Cards, keys and other things inside. First person to describe the contents accurately will have it. Ask inside shop.

LOST
I have lost my wallet with £30 in cash and credit card inside. Also photo of cat. Reward: £10.

Phone: 0795 623487

2 Read the list of personal objects below. Put the objects in order according to how inconvenient it would be to lose each one (1 = most inconvenient; 10 = least inconvenient).

house keys ■ folding umbrella ■ theatre tickets ■ £100 in cash ■ diary ■ student card ■ £5 in cash
hotel room key ■ mobile phone ■ credit card

3 🔊 1.10 Listen to a man telling a story about an object he lost. What did he lose? How important was it?

Informal speech: using signpost phrases

1 🔊 1.10 Listen again and match each phrase a–d from the story with the correct function 1–4.

   a I should say
   b How shall I put it?
   c Now, where was I?
   d Let me see,

   1 returning to the subject
   2 gaining thinking time
   3 emphasizing a point
   4 searching for a word

> **Technique**
>
> Use these phrases when necessary. They are *discourse markers*. They are correct English in informal and semi-formal speech, e.g. in the IELTS Speaking module. Then, make sure you continue to speak fluently.

18

The importance of the past

Planning your talk in Part 2

1 The task card below is taken from Speaking Part 2. Read the card and answer questions a–c below.

> Describe an important possession that you lost.
>
> You should say
>
> what the possession you lost was
>
> where you lost the possession
>
> what efforts you made to find it
>
> and explain why the possession was important to you.

   a What is the main topic?
   b How many separate instructions are there?
   c How many instructions relate to the future? How many relate to the past?

2 The notes below were made by a student who was preparing to give a talk on the topic in the card above. Which instructions on the card does each note relate to?

```
1 → shop              5 cards
2 → police            6 → newspaper
3 bag – shoulder strap  7 ? shop
4 handbag
```

> **Technique**
> Plan your talk by writing down a list of key words (around ten) and talk around them. You have only one minute to think and make notes.

3 Imagine you are the student who wrote the notes in exercise 2. Practise giving a short talk using the notes. Use some of the phrases below to help you.

Well, I should say first that   Finally, I
To find it, I first   Looking back, I realize that
After that, I   In future I will/won't

> **Technique**
> Finish your talk by looking to the future and talking about how you may want to do things differently. This gives you more to talk about. Sometimes you can talk about the precautions you may take.

4 Take one minute to think and make notes about your own talk on this topic, using your own experience. Then practise speaking for two minutes using your notes.

Describing precautions

1 Read the example sentence below. Underline the phrase which indicates that it is a precaution.

Example
In future, I will put labels on my suitcases in case they get lost on the plane.

2 Match each precaution a–f below with a situation 1–6 that it might prevent. Rewrite the sentences using the structure in exercise 1.

   a Keep some keys in a flowerpot in the front garden.
   b Keep a paper map in the car.
   c Note the phone number of your embassy.
   d Put a second umbrella in the car.
   e Bring a packet of sweets.
   f Write down the phone number of your bank.

   1 You lose your house keys.
   2 You lose your passport.
   3 Your GPS gives you wrong information.
   4 You lose your credit card.
   5 Your ears start to pop in the plane.
   6 You leave yours at home.

19

Unit 2

3 The task card below is taken from Speaking Part 2. Take a minute to think and make notes. Then practise speaking for two minutes.

> Describe a time when you were late for an event.
> You should say
> - what kind of event you were late for
> - what caused you to arrive late
> - what happened to you when you arrived
>
> and explain what you have learned from the experience.

Technique
Speak for 1½–2 minutes in Part 2 of the Speaking module.

Pronunciation: linking in connected speech

1 a 🔊 1.11 Listen to these pairs of words. In some pairs you can hear the sound /r/. In some, you cannot. If you can hear the sound, link the words like this 'four~apples'.

> car engine ■ car mechanic ■ rare opportunity ■ rare stamp ■ amateur actor ■ amateur dramatics
> summer activity ■ summer clothes ■ for ever ■ for now ■ fire escape ■ fire alarm

b Say the phrases yourself, putting in the links where needed.

2 a 🔊 1.12 Listen to these phrases. In each phrase there is a link. In another part of the phrase, a sound is dropped. Mark in the link and cross out the dropped sound.

> bigger and better ■ more and more ■ quicker and quicker ■ wider and longer

b Say the phrases, putting in the links and dropping the sounds.

3 a 🔊 1.13 Listen to these phrases. The phrases all have links. Write /w/ (as in *wet*) or /j/ (as in *yet*) to show the link.

Examples   zoo entry → zoo (**w**) entry
            coffee evening → coffee (**j**) evening

> nearly always ■ key ingredient ■ new idea ■ every opportunity ■ too easy ■ very often

b Say the phrases yourself, putting in the links.

4 a 🔊 1.14 Listen to these phrases. Mark the links in the phrases by inserting /dʒ/ (as in *judge*) or /tʃ/ (as in *church*).

Examples   can't you → can't /tʃ/ you
            could you → could /dʒ/ you

> not yet ■ told you so ■ not usually ■ not yours ■ mind you ■ heard you the first time

b Say the phrases yourself, putting in the links.

5 🔊 1.15 Listen to a candidate answering a Part 2 task about an embarrassing occasion. Mark where the links in these sentences should go.

This happened about a year ago (r). I had chosen a pullover in a shop (r). I joined the queue at the cash desk (w). 'Could you put the card in the machine, please?' the shop assistant said (dʒ). I looked for my card but I couldn't find it. 'I know I had it yesterday,' I thought (tʃ). My face became redder and redder (r). I said, 'I'm sorry about this. I'll leave the pullover here (j).' I rushed out of the store, very embarrassed (j).

Technique
Make links between the words as you speak. This helps your English sound natural. It also gets you a better grade for fluency in connected speech.

6 Say the sentences in exercise 5, putting in the links.

20

The importance of the past

Exam listening

Section 3

🔊 1.16

Questions 21–25

*Complete the sentences below. Write **NO MORE THAN TWO WORDS AND/OR A NUMBER** for each answer.*

The name of the assignment is 'Museums – their **21** .... and

.... '.

The number one problem with local museums is **22** ....

The purpose of the museum shop is to **23** ....

The boat was approximately **24** .... years old.

The **25** .... are dark.

🔊 1.17

Questions 26–30

How does Tom think the museums should be funded?

A by the state

B by local government

C by private funding

*Write the correct letter **A**, **B** or **C** next to Questions 26–30.*

26 local history museums   ....

27 natural history museums ....

28 science museums   ....

29 craft museums   ....

30 working farms   ....

3 Machines, cycles and processes

UNIT AIMS

LISTENING SKILLS
Understanding information in flow charts

SPEAKING SKILLS
Answering Part 3 discussion questions
Introducing opinions
Pronunciation: using opinion phrases

Topic talk

1 Predict how items a–c bought on the Internet might be damaged in the post. Use these words to help you:

> damaged ■ broken ■ torn ■ ripped

2 Answer the questions a–d.
  a Is it safe to shop over the Internet?
  b What do you think the main effects of Internet shopping are?
  c Have you bought anything over the Internet? If not, would you?
  d Have you ever bought anything which was damaged? What did you do?

3 Match the problems to one of the pictures in exercise 1.
  a The lens is scratched.
  b There's something wrong with the lid.
  c The lens cover is missing.
  d The zoom lens doesn't work.

4 Which of the materials below can be categorized as (a) cloth, (b) metal, or (c) man-made?

> fur ■ gold ■ cotton ■ wood ■ linen ■ polyester ■ aluminium ■ silk ■ brass
> glass ■ plastic ■ tin ■ leather ■ steel

5 Name a common object which you would use the words below to describe.
  Example
  spherical: football

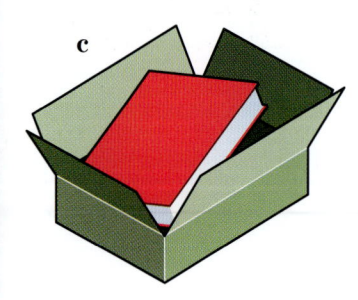

> spherical ■ rectangular ■ square ■ circular ■ oval ■ spiral

6 In the IELTS Speaking Part 2, you may have to describe an object that you like, such as a camera or a tablet. Describe an object that you have bought in your own words, without saying its name. Ask another student to guess what the object is.

> **Technique**
> Create a list of objects that you like and dislike and a few ways to describe them physically.

Machines, cycles and processes

7 In Listening Section 1, you may hear a conversation between a customer and a shop assistant. Match the complaints about the objects in 1–8 with the product details a–h.

1 I bought this software CD and it won't work.
2 There is something wrong with the frame of my sunglasses.
3 I can't get the TV to work properly.
4 I'm ringing to complain about the vase you sent.
5 The box had a 'handle with care' sticker on it, but it was torn.
6 The tablet won't switch on.
7 I washed this jumper.
8 The book got here on time, but it was damaged.

a And when I looked inside the contents were crushed and broken.
b The arms are too tight.
c When it arrived, the cover was ripped.
d I think the connection is loose.
e The picture only appears in black and white.
f When it arrived, it had completely shattered.
g I get an error message, and it just keeps jamming in the machine.
h And it has just fallen apart.

> **Technique**
> Make a list of words and phrases related to problems and breakages, etc.

8 Complete the table below with a possible fault from the list. You may use each word only once.

wobbly ▪ ripped ▪ uncomfortable ▪ snapped ▪ jammed ▪ cracked scratched ▪ twisted ▪ faded ▪ leaking

	Object	Component	Fault
a	trousers	leg	_____
b	food blender	bowl	_____
c	backpack	zip	_____
d	sweatshirt	colour	_____
e	mirror	glass	_____
f	sandals	strap	_____
g	CD	surface	_____
h	bicycle	seat	_____
i	memory stick	prong	_____
j	table	leg	_____

9 Make sentences using ideas from exercise 8. Use the sentences below and add appropriate adverbs from the list.

very ▪ badly ▪ severely ▪ completely ▪ slightly

a You sent me this/these _____ and I was really annoyed to find that …
b When I opened the _____ you sent, I found the …

Unit 3

Listening skills Understanding information in flow charts

1 The flow chart below is used by a mail order company. It shows how staff should deal with customer queries. Put a–d in the correct spaces on the flow chart.

   a Ask purpose of customer's call
   b Request to place order
   c Put customer on hold
   d Can query be dealt with over telephone?

> **Technique**
> Practise reading and understanding flow charts. They can appear in the Listening and Reading Modules.

DEALING WITH TELEPHONE QUERIES

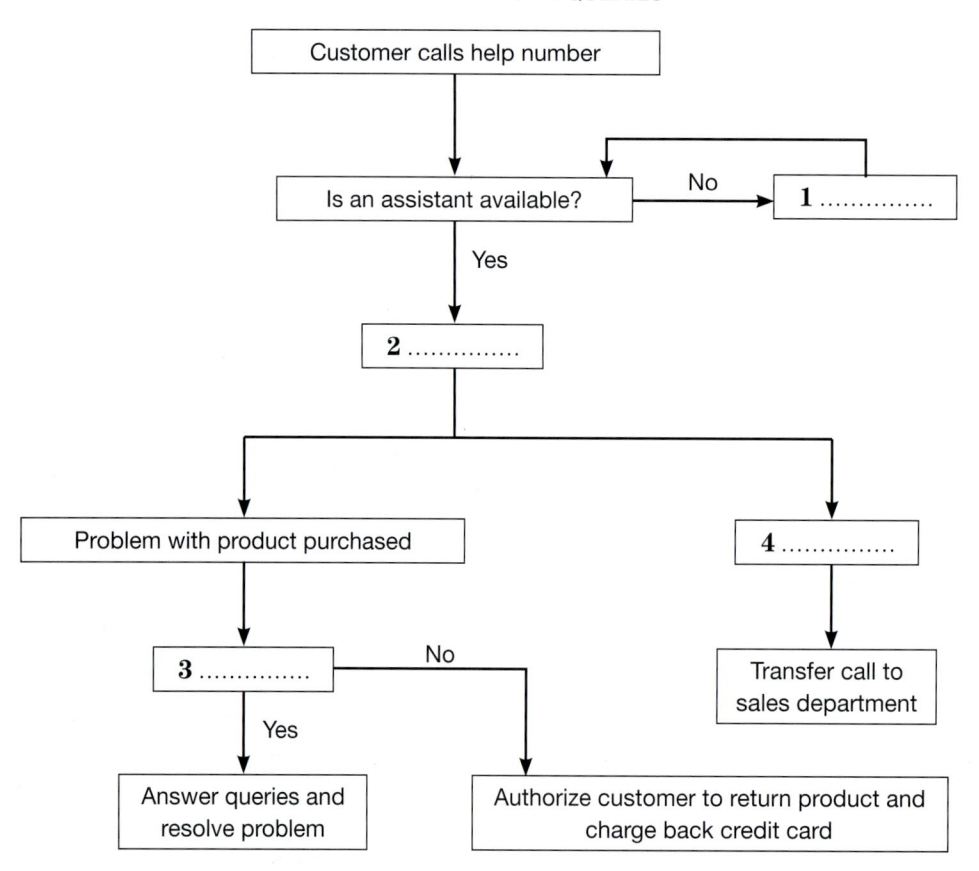

```
        Customer calls help number
                    │
                    ▼
          Is an assistant available? ──No──▶  1 ............
                    │                              │
                   Yes                             │ (loop back)
                    ▼
               2 ............
                    │
         ┌──────────┴──────────┐
         ▼                     ▼
  Problem with product      4 ............
  purchased                    │
         │                     ▼
         ▼              Transfer call to
     3 ............ ──No──┐   sales department
         │                │
        Yes               ▼
         ▼         Authorize customer to return product and
  Answer queries and      charge back credit card
  resolve problem
```

2 A flow chart in an IELTS Listening task shows that information is related in particular ways. Label each phrase in the box below with the relationship it indicates. Choose from: *cause and effect*, *conditional* or *linear ordering*.

> As a result ■ This means that ■ If … , then ■ Firstly ■ Otherwise ■ Next ■ Unless … , then
> This leads to ■ Finally ■ If not, then ■ To begin with

3 Imagine that a training manager is describing the procedure above for dealing with customer queries. Which phrases from exercise 2 would you expect to hear? Write the phrases on the flow chart near the relevant boxes.

4 The information opposite is taken from a flow chart task. Answer questions a–d.
   a What is the starting point and end point of the process?
   b What is the general topic?
   c Which nouns appear many times in the chart?
   d Which words from exercise 2 above do you expect to hear and where?

24

Machines, cycles and processes

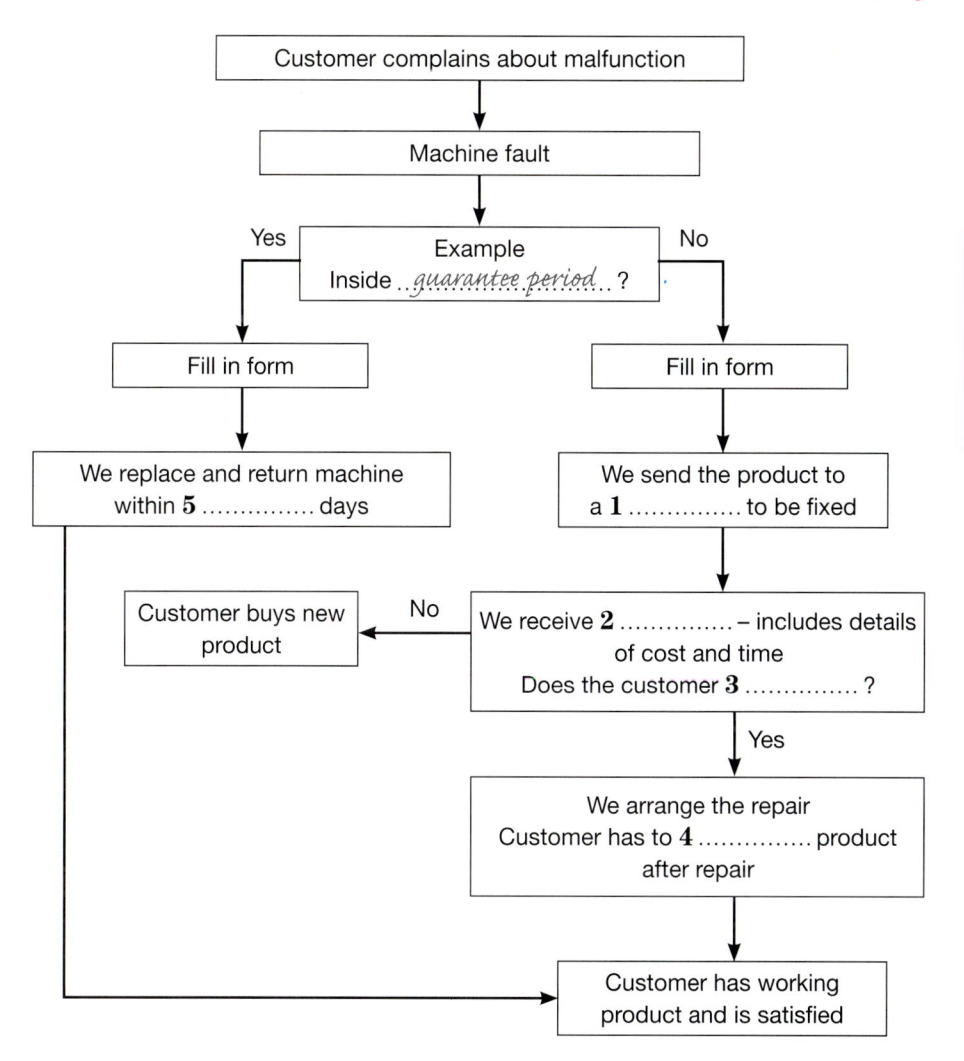

```
Customer complains about malfunction
              ↓
        Machine fault
              ↓
   Yes ← Example → No
        Inside *guarantee period* ?
    ↓                        ↓
Fill in form            Fill in form
    ↓                        ↓
We replace and return    We send the product to
machine within          a 1 .............. to be fixed
5 .............. days           ↓
                    We receive 2 .............. – includes details
          No ←     of cost and time
Customer buys          Does the customer 3 .............. ?
new product                     ↓ Yes
                    We arrange the repair
                    Customer has to 4 .............. product
                    after repair
                                ↓
              Customer has working
              product and is satisfied
```

> **Technique**
> Read the flow chart quickly and carefully. It gives you information about what you will hear in the Listening task.

5 🔊 **1.18** Listen to the first part of the recording and complete the gaps in the flow chart. Write NO MORE THAN TWO WORDS OR A NUMBER for each answer.

6 🔊 **1.19** The form below is taken from a form completion task. It follows on from the flow chart in exercise 5. Listen to the recording and complete the form. Write ONE WORD OR A NUMBER for each answer.

Harvey's Homewares

Faulty Product Replacement Instruction
Product Make: Gleeware
Model: Breadmaker 3
Model No: **6** ....
Shop where bought: Bluewater
Date of purchase: 2.12.13
Customer surname: **7** .... Initials: J.H
House number: **8** .... Road name: **9** .... Gardens
Postcode: AD22 4SC
Day of delivery: **10** ....

25

Unit 3

Speaking skills Answering part 3 discussion questions

1 There are many influences on the way people shop. Number each factor below 1–8 according to how much you think it influences what you buy (1 = most important; 8 = least important).

> advertising ■ convenience ■ fashion ■ luxury
> necessity ■ quality ■ shop service ■ value for money

2 For each of the factors you rated 1, 2 and 3 above, think of a purchase you made where that factor influenced you. Tell another student about this experience.

3 Statements a–h below relate to the topic of shopping. Decide which of the statements you agree and disagree with.
  a Shopping habits have been changed by globalization.
  b Shopping can be a form of relaxation.
  c The Internet will eventually mean the end of shopping as we know it.
  d People worldwide are becoming more materialistic.
  e Shopping today is a less personal process than shopping in the past.
  f The purpose of advertising is to inform people about what is available.
  g Discarded packaging is causing serious environmental problems.
  h Shopping in local markets is preferable to shopping in big stores.

4 Speaking Part 3 discussion questions are often formed in predictable ways. Match the beginning of questions 1–8 to their endings a–h.
  Example
  1f In what ways have shopping habits been changed by globalization?

1	In what ways have	a	of advertising?
2	To what extent is shopping a form of	b	becoming more materialistic?
3	To what degree will the Internet	c	a less personal activity than shopping in the past?
4	To what extent are people worldwide	d	relaxation?
5	In what ways is shopping today	e	mean the end of shopping as we know it?
6	What is the purpose	f	shopping habits been changed by globalization?
7	In what ways does	g	in local markets or shopping in big stores?
8	Which do you prefer, shopping	h	discarded packaging cause environmental problems?

Technique

Answer Part 3 questions by expressing opinions, justifying opinions, describing, comparing and analysing. Part 3 is about abstract issues.

Machines, cycles and processes

5 🔊 1.20 Listen to three people answering questions on the topics in exercise 4. Identify which topic they are discussing and write the question they are answering in the spaces below.

Speaker 1: _____

Speaker 2: _____

Speaker 3: _____

6 Give your own answer to one of the questions in exercise 4.

Introducing opinions

1 🔊 1.20 Listen again. For each speaker, make a note of the phrases they use to introduce their opinions.

Speaker 1: _____

Speaker 2: _____

Speaker 3: _____

2 With a partner, ask and answer the questions you wrote in exercise 4 in the previous section. Use the phrases below to introduce your own opinions.

Phrase bank
In my view/opinion,
Well, from my point of view,
To my mind,
It seems to me that
Personally, I think
My impression is that
I suppose

Technique
Use phrases like these in Part 3. They show that you are able to communicate your own ideas effectively. Try not to repeat a phrase: use a range of phrases.

3 Read the three short texts about fashion. To what extent do you agree with the ideas expressed?

The fashion cycle

As everyone knows, what's in fashion today was probably in fashion twenty years ago. However, cheap imported clothes have meant that the fashion cycle is getting shorter and shorter. In the past, people looked after their clothes and repaired them when necessary. Today, people change the clothes and outfits they wear more regularly, and the media and advertisers encourage them to do this.

You are what you wear

A generation ago, what teenagers wore to school was not a matter of choice. They had to wear a uniform. To some extent, the same was true of adults who wore serious business suits in the office. Nowadays, things are rather different: schoolchildren can customize their uniform; adults have dress-down days. More often we choose exactly what we wear, and with this has come more anxiety about looking good and creating the right impression.

27

Unit 3

Keeping up with the Joneses

When people talk about fashion, they often have clothes in mind, but, in a way, fashion affects all aspects of our lives. People spend money on redecorating their houses, on eating organic food or on the latest four-wheel-drive car because they perceive these things to be fashionable, not because they need them. That's not a criticism, it's just human nature.

Technique

Talk about people or society in general in Part 3. Use your own experience as an example, but return to talk again about the general topic. In Part 1 you can personalize; in Part 3 you should generalize.

4 Match each text with one of the Speaking Part 3 questions a–c below.
   a In what ways does fashion affect different aspects of our lives?
   b What makes people follow fashion?
   c To what extent does how we dress indicate who we are?

5 With another student, ask and answer the questions in exercise 4. Give your own views.

Pronunciation: using opinion phrases

1 Read these opinions about advertising. Underline the main stress in the phrases in italics.
   a *In my view*, there is too much advertising on television.
   b *To my mind*, advertising is fun.
   c *It seems to me* that advertising does more harm than good.
   d *My impression is* that most advertising is misleading.

Technique

Pause briefly after saying one of these phrases, to give emphasis and to collect your thoughts before carrying on with your opinion.

2 1.21 Listen to the recording and review your answer. Which word carries the main stress in each phrase?

3 Give your opinion on these statements, using the phrases above.
   a Internet shopping is a great thing.
   b Fashions change too quickly.
   c Excessive packaging of products like groceries should be prohibited.
   d Shopping is hard work.

Machines, cycles and processes

Exam listening

Section 4
🔊 1.22

Questions 31–35

Complete the sentences below.

*Write **ONE WORD ONLY** for each answer.*

Recycling is principally the responsibility of **31** ....

The second stage in the cycle relates to **32** .... in general.

Harvesting includes cutting down trees and **33** ....

Chemical processes create **34** ....

A significant proportion of the **35** .... stage is unnecessary.

Questions 36–40

Complete the flow chart.

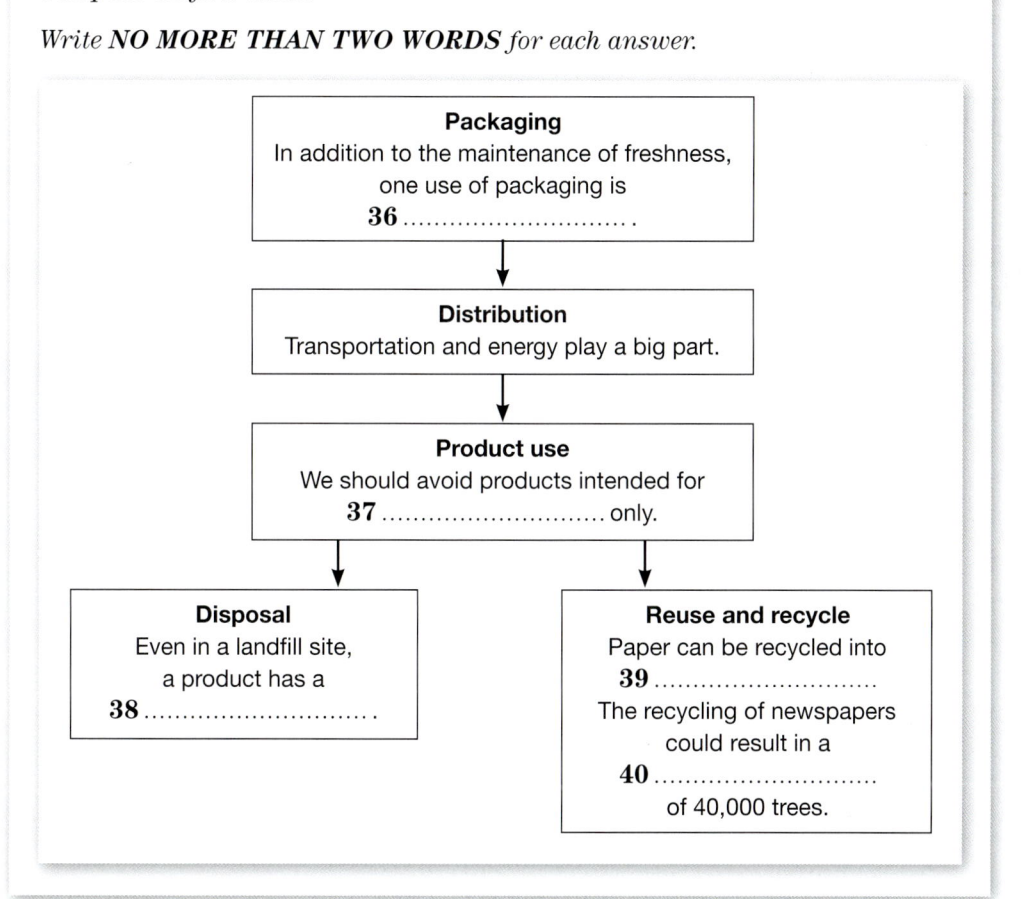

*Write **NO MORE THAN TWO WORDS** for each answer.*

Packaging
In addition to the maintenance of freshness, one use of packaging is
36 ....

↓

Distribution
Transportation and energy play a big part.

↓

Product use
We should avoid products intended for
37 .... only.

↓   ↓

Disposal
Even in a landfill site, a product has a
38 ....

Reuse and recycle
Paper can be recycled into
39 ....
The recycling of newspapers could result in a
40 ....
of 40,000 trees.

4 Education

UNIT AIMS

LISTENING SKILLS
Identifying campus contexts
Using information in multiple-choice questions
Answering summary completion questions

SPEAKING SKILLS
Describing people
Making notes
Pronunciation: placing stress in compound nouns

Topic talk

1 Look at the photo and answer the questions below.

    a Is the situation in the photo a tutorial, a seminar or a lecture? What is the difference?
    b Which of the three modes of teaching do you think is the best way of learning?
    c What are the similarities or differences between teaching in universities in your home country and other parts of the world like the UK?

2 Listening Section 3 often relates to academic courses. Complete the sentences below about courses with nouns from the list.

> requirements ■ analysis ■ criteria ■ dissertation ■ essay ■ evaluation
> module ■ paper ■ portfolio ■ programme

    a In order to study photography, you have to fulfil the *course* _____ , which include a foundation qualification in art.
    b Many people fail at medicine due to the difficulty of meeting the *assessment* _____ .
    c Most mature students enrol on a *part-time* _____ .
    d At the start of each academic year, students choose which *core* _____ they will take.
    e As part of their jobs, many lecturers are expected to submit at least one *academic* _____ per year.
    f Students on the fine art programme are required to present a _____ *of their work*.
    g After collecting your data, you will need to carry out an *in-depth* _____ of it.
    h To get a good mark, students should show they are capable of making a *critical* _____ of the literature.
    i At the end of the course, each student must submit a 4,000-word *long* _____ .
    j After you have submitted your *MA* _____ , you will have to wait about four months for your final grade.

Technique

Keep a record of words related to themes such as education. Make sure you keep an example of the context the word is used in. You can also put the words onto revision cards.

Education

3 Look at the sentences in exercise 2 again. Which verb comes before the noun phrase in each case?

4 Decide which noun phrase in exercise 2 contains
  a adjective + noun, e.g. *part-time programme*
  b noun + noun, e.g. *course requirements*

> **Technique**
> Record examples of the verb and noun phrases (adjective + noun and noun + noun) for your future reference.

5 The steps a–g below give details of how to prepare a piece of written work as part of a course. Work with another student. Put the steps in a logical order.
  a present an analysis of the data
  b include a bibliography
  c describe the methods used for collecting data
  d set out your hypothesis and explain your terms of reference
  e draw conclusions based on your analysis
  f provide a survey of existing literature
  g state your aims and objectives

6 The statements a–j below were made by students about courses they are taking. Check the meaning of each phrase and then complete the statements with a feature from the list.

> research project ■ deadlines ■ easy-going tutors
> end-of-year examination ■ background reading list
> extensions ■ weekly seminars ■ individual tuition
> ongoing assessment ■ practical work ■ vocational content

  a The tutors provide you with a _____ before the course.
  b As part of our assessment, we have to plan and carry out a _____ .
  c It's a very flexible programme: we have very _____ .
  d It can get very stressful: we are assessed by _____ .
  e Coursework has really fixed _____ . You can't get _____ .
  f Everyone gets _____ if they are experiencing difficulties.
  g The course is marked by _____ of written work.
  h I spend a lot of time doing _____ in a laboratory.
  i It's mostly _____ : it will all be useful for my career.
  j There are regular _____ in which people take turns to make presentations.

7 With a partner, discuss these questions about the statements in exercise 6.
  a Which statements would attract you to take a course? Which would put you off?
  b Have you had experiences similar to these? If so, tell your partner about what happened to you.

8 Make a list of situations and processes related to education and update it as you prepare for the IELTS, e.g. *lectures, tutorials, seminars, presentations.* Keep words and phrases related to these situations, e.g. *listen to/attend a lecture, make a presentation.*

Unit 4

Listening skills Identifying campus contexts

1 Listening Section 3 is normally set in a place of academic study. Complete each list below with nouns that you normally associate with them. Some examples are given in italics.

- **a** library — *journals,*
- **b** student flat — *study bedroom,*
- **d** lecture theatre — *aisles,*
- **e** laboratory — *experiment,*

2 Look at the first two multiple-choice questions in exercise 1 below. What words in the questions might help you to get the correct answers? Predict what the answers might be.

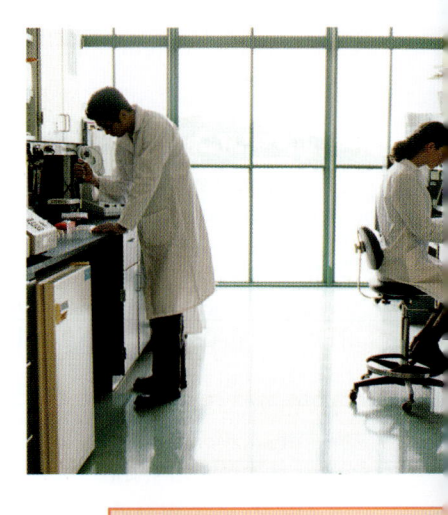

Using information in multiple-choice questions

1 The questions below are taken from a multiple-choice task. Read multiple-choice questions 1–4 and answer questions a–d.
- **a** How many speakers do you think you will hear?
- **b** Who has to do assignments?
- **c** Which academic subject do you think they are studying?
- **d** What area of that subject are they focusing on?

> **Technique**
> Use the information in the questions to give you an idea of what you will hear. You will not be able to guess the answers, but you will be able to predict the themes and topics of the passage.

---

1 Where are the speakers having this discussion?

  A a library

  B a student flat

  C a lecture theatre

2 How has Chloe spent the morning?

  A drinking coffee

  B training

  C studying

3 According to Bill, what does the experiment show?

  A Quantities of water are hard to measure.

  B Children under five make many mistakes.

  C Clear thinking is difficult for small children.

4 Bill's assignment is about the stages in a child's

  A emotional development.

  B mental development.

  C social development.

---

2 🔊 **1.23** Listen to the first part of this Listening Section 3 recording and answer Questions 1–4 in exercise 1, choosing the correct answer A, B or C.

Education

Answering summary completion questions

1 The list below gives eight popular degree subjects. Put them in order according to how easy or difficult you think each subject is (1 = easiest; 10 = most difficult).

> psychology ■ medicine ■ engineering ■ law ■ physics
> sociology ■ languages ■ sports science ■ business studies ■ fine art

2 Compare your answers with another student. Then answer the questions below.
  a Which of these subjects would you prefer to study? Why?
  b How far would you agree that the most popular subjects also tend to be the easiest?
  c Which subjects have you enjoyed studying most in the past? Why?

3 The paragraph below is taken from a summary completion task.
  a Which speaker does it concentrate on?
  b What aspect of her studies does it discuss?

Chloe started the psychology course in the **5** _____ year. Previously she studied law. She enjoyed studying the **6** _____ branch of that subject. The worst thing was having to remember lots of **7** _____ and _____ . She found **8** _____ especially technical. She did not enjoy spending her time reading about **9** _____ in the library. The part of the psychology course she likes best is experimental psychology, because it involves **10** _____ activities.

---

4 Match each of the predictions below with a gap in the paragraph in exercise 3. Think of any other predictions you can add.
  a It's an area of law, but it's technical, so maybe it's something like *property law*.
  b It's an area of law, and it's interesting, so maybe it's something like *family law*.
  c It's something that goes with activities, like *useful* or *difficult*.
  d This is something like *last*, or an ordinal number like *second*.
  e Something you have to remember, like *names* or *dates*.
  f It's something lawyers read about, like *judgements*.

> **Technique**
>
> Use the reading time to think about the overall topic of the summary. The general topic of each answer may be clear from the context.

5 🔊 1.24 Listen to the second recording and complete the summary. Write NO MORE THAN TWO WORDS for each answer.

33

Unit 4

Speaking skills   Describing people

1 Answer the questions below about the teachers you had at school.
   a   How well do you remember your teachers?
   b   Was there a teacher you especially liked? Why?
   c   How in general can teachers make lessons more interesting and fun? Is it important to do this? Is it always possible to do this?

2 Look at the list of qualities. Match them with the examples.

	Quality		Example	Importance
1	Audible	a	They avoid negative criticism.	
2	Demanding	b	They tell lots of jokes.	
3	Conscientious	c	They speak loudly.	
4	Positive	d	They do not allow talking or playing in class.	
5	Polite	e	They give a lot of praise.	
6	Knowledgeable	f	They play competitive sport.	
7	Strict	g	They mark and return students' work quickly.	
8	Physically fit	h	They know everything about their subject.	
9	Generous	i	They always say 'please' and 'thank you'.	
10	Humorous	j	They set high standards.	

> **Technique**
>
> Use an adjective to describe someone, and then follow it with a description of what he or she does. For example, 'Miss Jones was very strict – she insisted that every student put their hand up before asking a question and …'.

3 a Decide how important each quality is: put I (Important), U (Useful) or N (Not Important) in the third column.

   b Are there any other qualities you would add to the list? Give the adjective and an example.

4 🔊 1.25 The task card below is taken from Speaking Part 2. Listen to a person talking about the topic on the task card. Make a brief note on the card of the answers they give to each prompt.

Describe a teacher you can remember from your schooldays.

You should say
   what subjects they taught
   what this teacher looked like
   what kind of person they were

and explain how this person has influenced you.

Education

5 Match each phrase in the list to one of the functions a–d.
  a Introducing your choice.
  b Explaining the reason for your choice.
  c Describing physical features.
  d Describing character.

Physically, he/she was …
The … I've chosen is …
What … taught me was that …
In terms of personality, …
I can remember … really well.
He/she looked …
Character-wise, he/she was …
I'll never forget him/her because …

> **Technique**
> Use these phrases to structure your talk. Use them when you are moving from one point to the next.

6 🔊 1.25 Listen again. Which phrases from exercise 5 does the speaker use?

7 Take one minute to think and make notes for your own talk on this topic, using your own experience. Then practise speaking for two minutes using your notes and the phrases in exercise 5.

Making notes

1 Another student made the notes below for the Speaking Part 2 task card in exercise 4. Add the words in the list below to the appropriate part of the diagram.

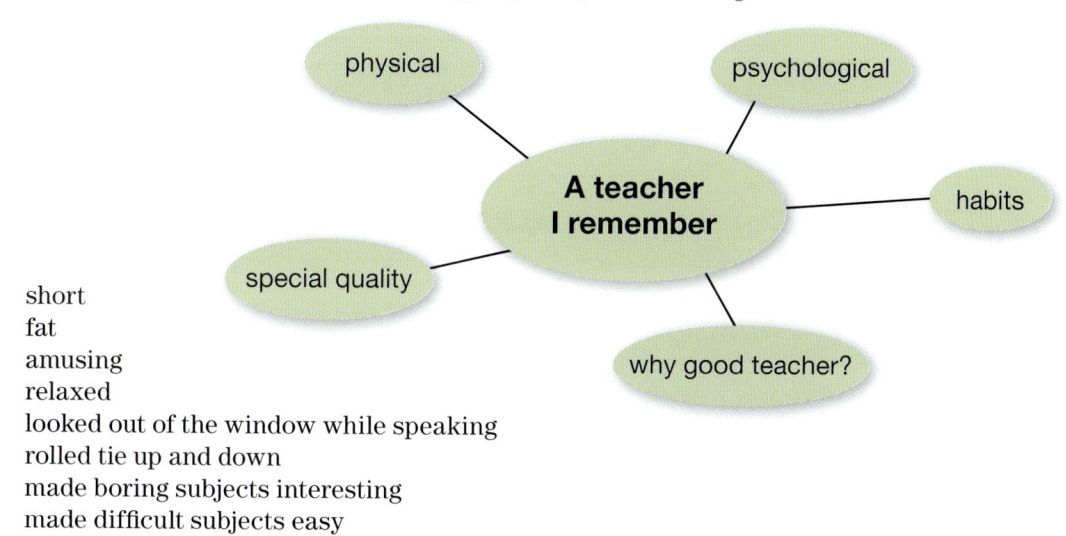

Diagram centre: **A teacher I remember**, connected to: physical, psychological, habits, why good teacher?, special quality

short
fat
amusing
relaxed
looked out of the window while speaking
rolled tie up and down
made boring subjects interesting
made difficult subjects easy
cheerful personality

2 Lists A and B below describe the advantages and disadvantages of different ways of making notes. Answer questions a–c.
  a Which list relates to the technique in exercise 1?
  b What kind of note-taking does the other list describe?
  c Which method of making notes would work best for you?

> **Technique**
> Use organic notes (like in this example) or linear notes. Use the kind you prefer and that does not take a lot of time in the exam.

List A
encourages creative thinking
many ways through the ideas
takes little time to write
uses very few words
can be messy

List B
encourages logical thinking
one way through the ideas
can take a long time to write
uses more words
very tidy

35

Unit 4

3 Using the note-taking technique you prefer, make notes on the Speaking Part 2 task card below, using your own experience. Then practise speaking for two minutes using your notes.

> Describe a person you know who has helped you in some way.
>
> You should say
>
> how you know this person
>
> what abilities this person has
>
> when this person first helped you
>
> and explain how this help has influenced your life.

Pronunciation: placing stress in compound nouns

1 Look at these words connected with education. Mark the stressed syllable by putting the stress mark ' before the stressed syllable. The first one has been done for you.

- a 'article
- b assistant
- c journal
- d tutor
- e registration
- f library
- g lecturer
- h security
- i seminar

2 🔊 1.26 Listen to the recording and put the words you hear into the right box. The first two have been done for you.

Column 1: two words, one main stress	Column 2: two words, two stresses
law tutor	*young tutor*

3 Which column is the one with compound nouns? From looking at the columns, where is the main stress in compound nouns?

Delete as appropriate, to form the correct rules:

a In *compound nouns/other combinations* the main stress is on the first word.

b In *compound nouns/other combinations* there is a stress on each word.

4 🔊 1.27 Jack and Georgina are university students. They meet on campus. Listen to the dialogue and fill in the gaps using the compound nouns in the box. Then practise the dialogue.

> lecture theatre ■ help desk ■ seminar room ■ revision class ■ library card

Jack: Where are you going? To the **1** _____ ?

Georgina: No, a **2** _____ . It's in **3** _____ number six.

Jack: Oh right. Hope it's useful. I've lost my **4** _____ . I'm going to the **5** _____ to see if I can get a new one.

Georgina: Good luck. See you later.

Education

Exam listening

Section 4
🔊 1.28

Questions 31–35

Choose the correct letter **A, B** *or* **C**.

31 How long would terms be under the six-term system?

  A six weeks
  B seven weeks
  C thirteen weeks

32 What would happen to the summer holiday?

  A It would disappear.
  B It would be shortened.
  C It would be lengthened.

33 How much was the average learning loss in the summer?

  A two weeks
  B three weeks
  C seven weeks

34 In which subject was learning loss greatest among disadvantaged children?

  A maths
  B reading
  C writing

35 According to Marchmont's research, in the six-term system pupils performed

  A better than under the existing system.
  B worse than under the existing system.
  C the same as under the existing system.

Technique
Before you listen, read the questions quickly and carefully. You will have 30 to 60 seconds to do this. Predict the topics and themes.

Questions 36–40

Complete the summary below. Write **NO MORE THAN TWO WORDS** *for each answer.*

The familiar school terms in use today originated when many people worked in 36 .... Also, because of the heat, teaching children in July and August was difficult before the invention of 37 .... A different approach can be provided by the 38 .... An important factor in the success of these is the small 39 .... Also, the element of 40 .... is usually present, which contributes greatly.

37

5 Youth

UNIT AIMS

LISTENING SKILLS
Understanding maps
Answering sentence and table completion questions

SPEAKING SKILLS
Describing jobs
Stating advantages and disadvantages
Pronunciation: stressing compound adjectives

Topic talk

1 Look at the picture and answer the questions below.

a Are all of the attributes below suitable for a youth worker? Why/Why not?
- being articulate
- being prepared to learn
- being full of energy
- being responsible
- being highly-motivated
- being experienced

b Is being a youth worker more suitable for a younger or an older person? Give reasons for your answer.

c Would you apply for a job like this? Why/Why not?

2 Match each criterion 1–9 with a list of adjectives a–i. The first one has been done for you.

1 appearance ___c___
2 intellectual ability _____
3 maturity of outlook _____
4 interpersonal skills _____
5 communication skills _____
6 willingness to learn _____
7 qualifications _____
8 attitude to work _____
9 skills and general ability _____

a sociable, friendly, likeable, personable
b articulate, outgoing, communicative, well-spoken
c well-dressed, neat, well-groomed, elegant
d conscientious, hardworking, dependable, reliable
e well-qualified, computer-literate, well-trained
f bright, quick, clever, intelligent
g skilled, able, capable, experienced
h responsible, mature, grown-up, independent
i enthusiastic, eager, dynamic, adaptable, flexible

Technique
Learn how to describe and listen to descriptions of people and their attributes. It helps for both the listening and speaking component of the IELTS exam.

3 Add each of the adjectives below to the appropriate list a–i in exercise 2. One adjective is used twice.

> trustworthy ■ lively ■ accomplished ■ approachable ■ smart ■ adult
> well-mannered ■ educated

Youth

4 The adjectives in the list below are opposites of those in the lists in exercise 2. Match each adjective with its opposite.

> apathetic ■ careless ■ childish ■ inarticulate ■ scruffy ■ slow ■ uneducated ■ unfriendly ■ inexperienced

5 Divide questions a–h below into these two categories: closed question (can be answered *yes* or *no*), open question (requires a fuller answer).

a Does a young worker nowadays need to be more qualified than in the past?
b Are young people more or less interested in finding a career than in the past?
c What difficulties do young people face in the changing world we live in?
d Do you generally find job interviews difficult?
e How do you think the work environment will be changed for future generations of young people?
f What can be done to overcome these difficulties?
g How does this differ from the past?
h Why/Why not?

6 In which part of the Speaking test, Part 1 or Part 3, would you expect to find the questions in exercise 5?

Technique
Learn to distinguish between different types of questions. They are often divided into open and closed categories. Closed questions can be answered *yes* or *no*, whereas open questions require a fuller answer. As you prepare for the exam, build up a bank of examples of open and closed questions in the listening and speaking component. Compile example answers to go with them. You can record these electronically or on cards.

7 Decide which questions in exercise 5 could be answered by beginning with the phrases below.

- There are many problems, but perhaps the greatest challenge is …
- The most likely development is that …
- By far the best way to tackle the situation is … because …
- The main difference is …

8 With a partner, ask and answer the questions in exercise 5. Use the phrases in exercise 7. Then develop your answers by using the following words to trigger and organize your ideas.

> As a result,   This is because   Firstly,
> But perhaps the best solution is to
> Another point that will stand out is
> This means that

Unit 5

Listening skills Understanding maps

1 Look at the map and answer the questions.
   a What is between the station and the town hall?
   b What is opposite the post office?
   c What is next to the cinema?

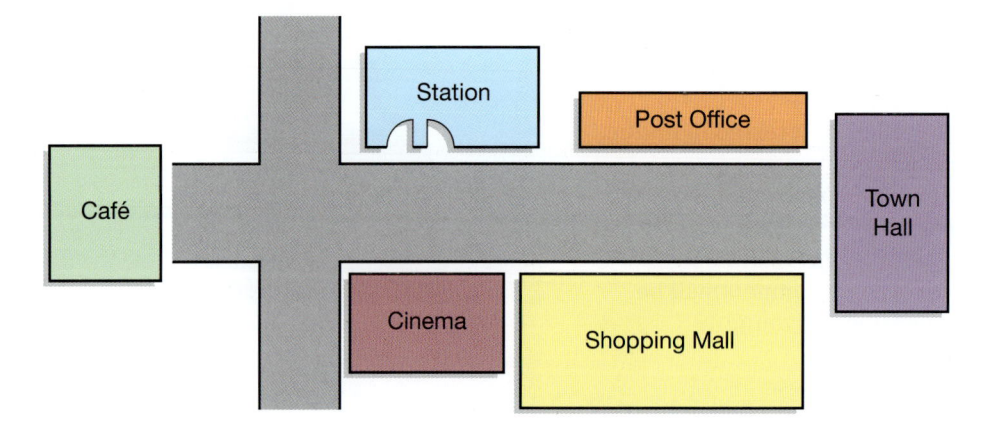

Technique
When you see a map question, run through all the words to describe position that you know. Common prepositions are *in front of*, *next to*, *behind*, *beside*, *opposite*, etc. You will probably hear some of them in the listening.

2 Look at the map again and match the sentence beginnings to the endings to make true statements. More than one ending is usually possible.

   1 Coming out of the station
   2 Leaving the town hall
   3 As you enter the town hall
   4 As you leave the café
   5 On your way into the café
   6 As you go into the station

   a the town hall is behind you.
   b the cinema is in front of you.
   c the post office is on your right.
   d the post office is on your left.
   e the post office is further away than the station.
   f the cinema is further away than the shopping mall.

3 Match the uses of *right* in these sentences with the correct meaning.
   1 The cinema is right in front of you.
   2 The post office is the right place to buy stamps.
   3 Coming from the café, the shopping mall is on your right.

   a correct
   b opposite of left
   c directly, immediately

4 The map on the next page is taken from a map-labelling task. Look at the map and answer questions a–d. Use these words in your answers:

   beside ■ near ■ between

   a Where is question 1 in relation to the food tent?
   b Where is question 2 in relation to campsite 1 and the disabled viewing?
   c Where is question 3 in relation to the stage and the bar?
   d Where is question 3 in relation to the disabled viewing?

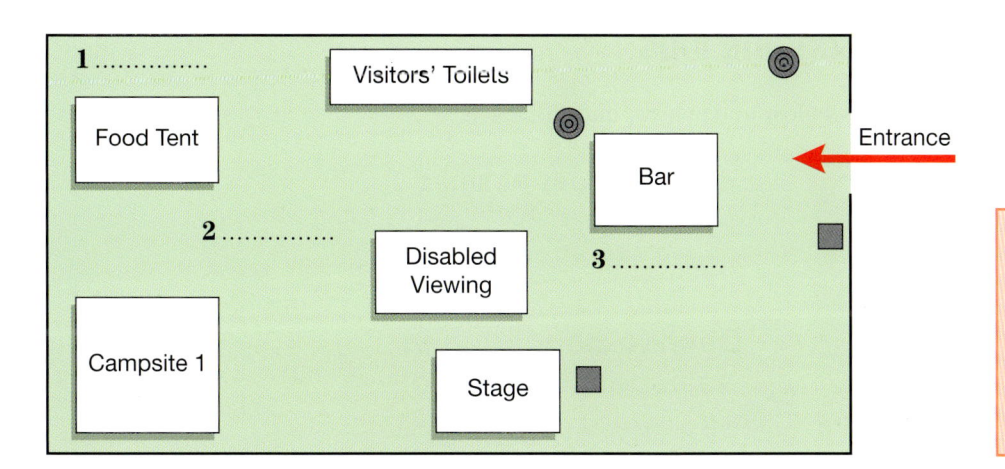

Youth

[Map: Food Tent, Visitors' Toilets, Bar, Entrance, Disabled Viewing, Campsite 1, Stage, with labels 1, 2, 3]

Technique
Look carefully at the map and ask yourself where things are in relation to the question numbers. Then listen for descriptions which match your ideas.

5 🔊 1.29 Listen to the first part of the recording and label the map. Write the correct letters A–F next to questions 1–3 on the map.

A small security office   D staff toilets
B main security office   E staff meeting point
C first aid tent   F visitors' meeting point

Answering sentence and table completion questions

1 Read the sentence and table completion questions which follow from the map-labelling task above. Then answer questions a–c below.

a What is the general theme of questions 4–6?
b Which questions in 4–6 relate to an event, a place and a thing?
c Which answers in the table are predictable, to some extent?

Technique
Check that you can find all the places on the map that the questions relate to. The information comes in the same order as the questions.

Complete the sentences below.

*Write **NO MORE THAN TWO WORDS** for each answer.*

4 In the first year, it was a ...., and not a real festival.
5 Shortly afterwards the event was moved, and the .... was in the background.
6 Now the festival is held in the ....

Complete the table below.

*Write **NO MORE THAN TWO WORDS AND/OR A NUMBER** for each answer.*

	Children's Zone team	Security team	First aid team
Meeting place	In Campsite 2	Behind the stage	8 At the ....
Meeting time	2 p.m.	7 .... p.m.	4 p.m.
Final meeting time for all teams	9 .... a.m.		
Final meeting place for all teams	10		

2 🔊 1.30 Listen to the second part of the recording and answer questions 4–10 in exercise 1.

41

Unit 5

Speaking skills Describing jobs

1 Read the small job advertisements below and answer questions a–e.

Men and women wanted for modelling
No experience necessary. Contracts with TV and magazines. £££
Phone 0789 345213

Fill envelopes at home
£4.50 per 100.
Phone 0766 657291

Waiters/waitresses wanted
Night work. Good pay plus tips.
Phone 0796 975779

Door-to-door kitchen salespeople wanted
Pay according to results.
Phone 0798 864233

   a Are these careers or jobs?
   b What, in your view, is the difference between a job and a career?
   c Which of these jobs is suitable for a student?
   d Which of these jobs would you be willing to do as a student?
   e What are the jobs that students do in your country?

2 Number the jobs in the list below according to how well-paid they are
(1 = highest paid; 4 = lowest paid) and according to how socially useful they are
(1 = most useful; 4 = least useful).

| bus driver ■ dentist ■ shop assistant ■ pop star |

3 Answer these questions about your answers in exercise 2.
   a Is the situation fair? Should the situation be different?
   b Should governments try to change the situation?

4 Which features from the list would you associate with each job a–h?
   a architect
   b nurse
   c company director
   d politician
   e doctor
   f schoolteacher
   g chef
   h footballer

| risk ■ excitement ■ social prestige ■ long holidays
long training ■ high job satisfaction
variety of job activities ■ high pay ■ good pension
social usefulness ■ expensive training |

Youth

Stating advantages and disadvantages

1 🔊 1.31 Listen to three people talking about jobs and answer the questions.
  a Which of them talk about working while studying?
  b Which of them talk about their own full-time job?
  c Which of them do not believe that working while studying is a good thing?

2 🔊 1.31 Answer questions a–i below with phrases from the list. Then listen again to the people speaking to check your answers.

First speaker
  a What phrase does he use to refer to advantages and disadvantages?
  b Which two phrases does he use to indicate a contrast?
  c How does he introduce his conclusion?

Second speaker
  d How does she introduce the disadvantages of her job?
  e How does she introduce the advantages of her job?
  f What word does she use to present her conclusion?

Third speaker
  g What phrase does she use instead of the *advantage*?
  h What phrase does she use instead of the *disadvantage*?
  i How does she introduce her conclusion?

> the minus ■ the disadvantage with … is that ■ weighing everything up
> the plus ■ on the other ■ pros and cons ■ overall ■ on balance
> the great advantage is that ■ on the one hand

Technique
Structure your answers in Part 3. Memorize phrases like these and use them as triggers to help you to give fuller and longer answers.

3 The ideas in the list below relate to the Speaking Part 3 question: *Is it better to go travelling on your own or with other people?* Which ideas relate to travelling alone? Which relate to travelling with others?

  a easier to make new friends
  b free to go where you please
  c complete control of your money
  d you must make group decisions
  e more safety in numbers
  f cheaper to share things
  g you may get lonely
  h you can stay extra time in places as you want
  i more fun

4 With a partner, give your own answer to the question in exercise 3. Use the expressions in the phrase bank below to help you.

> **Phrase bank**
> **Advantages**
> One definite plus is that
> The great advantage is
>
> **Disadvantages**
> One problem is that
> Another big disadvantage is
> A big minus is
> Balancing/Weighing everything up,
> On balance,
> Taking everything into account,

43

Unit 5

5 With a partner, ask and answer these Speaking Part 3 questions.
  a Is it a good idea to take a gap year after university and before starting a job?
  b When people are studying at university, is it better for them to live at home or to move away from their families?
  c Which is more important in a job, money or job satisfaction?
  d Which are more useful in helping people to relax – mental activities or physical activities?

Pronunciation: stressing compound adjectives

1 🔊 1.32 Where is the main stress on the word in bold in this sentence? Underline it.
The university has a **well-stocked** library. well OR stocked ?

What about this sentence?
The library is **well-stocked**. well OR stocked?

Listen and check your answer.

2 From your answer in exercise 1, can you state the rules? Delete as appropriate.
  a The main stress is usually on *the first/second* part of a compound adjective, when it comes before a noun.
  b The main stress is usually on *the first/second* part of a compound adjective, when it is alone, or after a verb.

3 🔊 1.33 A student is describing life at his university. The compound adjectives are in bold. Underline the main stress. The first one is done for you:

open-<u>mind</u>ed: *(main stress: mind)*

I like it here. The tutors are **open-minded** and **easy-going**. One or two of them are **world-famous**. I have to do a **thousand-word** essay every fortnight and there is an **end-of-year** exam. The **campus-based** accommodation is very good, although it is not cheap. Internet connection is provided, and there is a **user-friendly** student intranet. The town is **densely-populated** and has lots of nightlife. Life is **worry-free** here. I must go now – I've got an **hour-long** seminar to prepare for.

Listen and check your answers.

> **Technique**
> Use adjectives and phrases like these in answer to Part 1 questions.

4 Now read the passage aloud, putting the stress in the correct places.

5 Think of someone you know. Using the adjectives below, write sentences about him or her, changing the position of the adjective. Then practise saying the sentences.

| well-mannered ■ smartly-dressed ■ fair-minded ■ easy-going ■ quick-thinking |
| good-looking ■ well-travelled ■ warm-hearted ■ good-humoured ■ sports-mad |

> **Technique**
> Use adjectives like these for Part 2, if you are asked to describe someone you know.

Youth

Exam listening

Section 1

🔊 1.34

Questions 1–3

Label the map.

Choose answers from the list below. Write the correct letters A–H on the map.

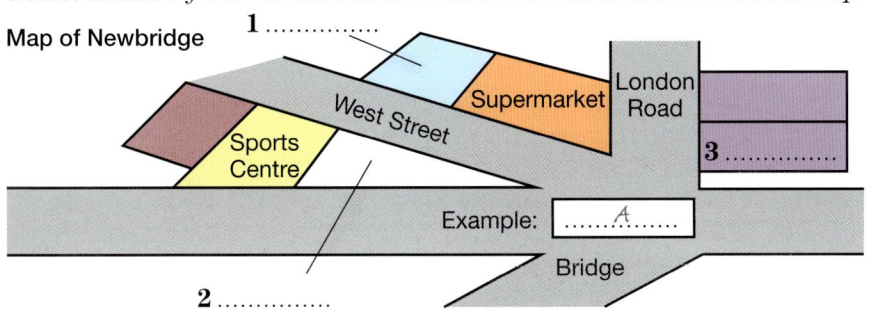

Map of Newbridge

A High Street (example)
B tennis courts
C car park
D The Towers
E The Heights
F railway station
G town hall
H bus station

Technique
Establish the starting point – the point from which the speaker gives directions.
Get this right and everything else will become clear.

🔊 1.35

Questions 4–8

Write the appropriate letters A–C against the flat numbers.

What is the next thing the student should do?

A apply to an agency
B enquire through the accommodation officer
C apply directly to the owner

4 Flat 4   ....
5 Flat 6   ....
6 Flat 8   ....
7 Flat 10 ....
8 Flat 14 ....

Questions 9 and 10

Complete the sentences below.

Write **NO MORE THAN TWO WORDS** for each answer.

The biggest employers in Newbridge used to be **9** ....

There is little student accommodation in the **10** .... around the town.

45

6 Culture

UNIT AIMS

LISTENING SKILLS
Understanding layout
Understanding noun phrases
Predicting from notes

SPEAKING SKILLS
Talking about free time activities
Expressing preferences
Dealing with unfamiliar topics
Pronunciation: shifting syllable stress

Topic talk

1 Look at the photo and answer the questions.

   a To what extent do buildings reflect the culture of a country?
   b How important is it to keep old buildings?
   c Which buildings are famous in your country?
   d How can we keep traditional buildings and still make progress?

2 In questions a–g, put the words in italics into the correct order.

   a *are / buildings / how / modern / popular* in your country? Why?
   b *same / architecture / is / the / the / as / here* in your home country?
   c *traditional / you / do / prefer / or / modern* architecture? Why?
   d *any / there / of / which / kind / is / building* you don't like? Why?
   e *you / buildings / special / have / of / significance / any / do* in your country?
   f *changed / type / the / of / building / has* since you were a child? How?
   g *building / kinds / of / what* appeal to you most? Why?

3 Match answers 1–7 below with questions a–g you made in exercise 2.

   1 I'm not too keen on tall structures like skyscrapers _____
   2 There are lots like the Parthenon _____
   3 I think I like more contemporary designs better _____
   4 Not at all. In fact, it couldn't be more different _____
   5 Buildings with lots of glass _____
   6 Only in recent years _____
   7 I'd say they are very much in fashion at the moment _____

Technique
Build your confidence in the speaking component of the IELTS exam by learning to process the examiner's questions quickly. Practise beginning to answer questions and then developing them.

46

Culture

4 Match responses 1–7 in exercise 3 with the explanations below which develop the answers.

a as new houses are appearing everywhere and old houses are being pulled down.
b because there are fewer mega-structures here, while in my country they are everywhere.
c because high buildings make me dizzy. I prefer buildings with three or four storeys.
d as old-fashioned buildings are dull and often a bit scary.
e which reflect the culture of the country and bring in tourists.
f as there was no money before, while now there's lots of investment.
g since they're brighter, which makes them more airy and cheerful.

5 With a partner, practise asking and answering the questions in exercise 2.

6 In Speaking Part 1, you may be asked to talk about your preferences. Complete sentences a–g with the words below.

> hate ■ adore ■ would rather ■ prefer ■ stand ■ appeal ■ dislike

a I don't _____ modern architecture, but I do think that there are many examples that are very ugly.
b I _____ live in town than in the countryside.
c I am fond of old family houses, but I _____ much more modern ones.
d I can't _____ old films except for early comedies.
e Books _____ to me as much as music.
f While some people simply _____ the theatre, I am indifferent to it.
g I don't _____ literature. It's just that I don't have much time for reading.

7 With a partner, express your preference out of each of the pairs of items below. Use the verbs in exercise 6 and explain your decisions.

a contemporary books or classic literature
b plays in the theatre or outdoor drama
c films at home or films in the cinema
d urban living or country life
e popular or classical music
f keeping a diary or writing a blog
g art films or Hollywood blockbusters

Unit 6

Listening skills Understanding layout

1 Two students attended a lecture on the attitudes of young people. Read the two sets of notes that they took. Then answer the questions below.

A
purpose of study
values among students
sample size
500 boys
aged 15
500 girls
same age
survey type
questions and answers

B
Values among young people
Purpose of study   a identification of values held by boys and girls
                    b differences between the two groups
Sample type   boys and girls (500 of each) 15 years
Name of study   relative values among adolescents
Survey type   Questionnaire
Items in survey
• money
• fashion
• success

> **Technique**
> Notice the different types of fonts used in complete the notes tasks. They tell you how the speaker will organize the information into main and subsidiary ideas.

a Which arrangement of notes is easier to understand?
b Which of the following are used to assist in the clear layout of the notes? Identify where they are used.

| italic type ■ bold ■ indentation ■ numbering/lettering ■ capitals ■ underlining ■ headings/titles |

2 Organize these notes about the country of Fiji in a clear and logical format. Use some of the features in exercise 1.

| capital ■ English ■ Fiji ■ official language ■ Suva ■ sugar ■ hot and wet ■ population ethnic composition ■ Fijian ■ coconuts ■ resources ■ Asian Indian ■ gold ■ 800,000 crops ■ climate ■ name of country |

Understanding noun phrases

1 Match the noun phrases in the box with the descriptions below.

| a holiday price comparison website ■ a cost-effective action plan
a celebrity gossip magazine ■ a child poverty report
a family shopping survey ■ a television drama newspaper review |

a A plan for action which is cost-effective.
b A survey asking about the shopping that families do.
c A magazine containing gossip about celebrities.
d A website which compares the prices of holidays.
e A report about poor children.
f A review in a newspaper of a drama which was shown on television.

Culture

2 What is the difference between the order of ideas in the descriptions and the order of the ideas in the noun phrases?

3 Create noun phrases from the words given at the end of the descriptions. The first one has been done for you.

- **a** A survey of the opinions of ordinary people.
  public opinion survey
- **b** The activity of collecting data from a survey.
  data/collection/survey
- **c** A timetable which a student has made to help him prepare for an exam.
  timetable/exam/preparation
- **d** A student who is studying engineering at Leeds University.
  student/Leeds University/engineering
- **e** A book which students can refer to about grammar.
  reference/grammar/book
- **f** An item of news about global warming.
  item/news/global warming

> **Technique**
> Watch out for noun phrases in Section 3 and Section 4. Sometimes the noun phrase will be in the question, sometimes in the Listening text. Use simple noun phrases in the Speaking module, too.

Predicting from notes

1 The notes below are taken from a note completion task based on a lecture. Read the task and answer these questions.
- **a** What is the title of the lecture?
- **b** How many parts are there to the lecture?
- **c** What is the subject of each part?
- **d** How does the lecture end?
- **e** What information can you predict for each space?

2 🔊 2.1 Listen to the recording and complete the notes. Write NO MORE THAN TWO WORDS AND/OR A NUMBER for each answer.

Culture and Society

Study: 2004
on the global teenager hypothesis (i.e. values of teenagers in the world are similar)
Is there a global culture?
One special aspect of the study: **1** .... in three cultures

Sample: **2** .... high school students
14–17 years
Three countries: China, Japan, USA

Questionnaire: number of statements: **3** ....

Three examples of statements:
Statement 1 It is really true that **4** .... can make you happy.
Statement 2 My life's dream is to own **5** ....
Statement 5 Having the right **6** .... is the most important thing in life.

Three examples of results
Statement 1 nationality agreeing most strongly: **7** ....
Statement 2 nationality agreeing most strongly: **8** ....
Statement 5 nationality agreeing most strongly: **9** ....

General conclusion
The global teenager hypothesis is **10** .... by this research.
More research needed!

Unit 6

Speaking skills Talking about free time activities

1 Read these two diaries written by the same person and answer questions a–d.

Saturday 16 March
a.m. 11.00 meet Ken in town – coffee
p.m. 2.30 golf with David at club
eve 7.30 cinema: Les Misérables
Meet the girls at 7.00 in the usual place.

Saturday 16 March
Ken was delayed so did shopping at the supermarket. Met him for lunch – he paid! Big rush to get to the club in time. David had brought Bill and Charlotte. We all played. I need a lot more practice! Only Janet arrived for the movie, so we went to see *Skyfall* instead. Great fun, better than *Les Misérables*, I imagine.

- **a** What are the differences between the two diaries?
- **b** Do you think her day was better than she had planned or not?
- **c** Is it better to make detailed plans for the future or to leave some things to chance?
- **d** What can be the disadvantages of planning ahead?

2 Put the leisure activities in the list into three groups 1–3. Some activities may appear in more than one group.

1 Sports
2 Hobbies
3 Social activities

> golf ■ ice hockey ■ chess ■ stamp-collecting ■ meeting friends ■ tennis ■ gardening
> going to concerts ■ going to parties ■ chatting on the phone ■ football ■ shopping

3 In Speaking Part 1, you may be asked about your leisure activities. Answer these questions about the activities in exercise 2.

- **a** Which of these, if any, do you like doing?
- **b** Are there other activities, hobbies or sports which take up a lot of your time?
- **c** To what extent do you plan how and when you do them?

> **Technique**
> Be ready to speak about your hobbies and social life in the Speaking module. Make a list of key points on these topics. Don't learn a 'speech' by heart.

Expressing preferences

1 🔊 2.2 Listen to three people talking about what they like doing in their free time. Complete the table below with the activities they like doing.
Which is their favourite?

	Activities	Favourite
Speaker 1:	_____	_____
Speaker 2:	_____	_____
Speaker 3:	_____	_____

2 🔊 2.2 Complete the lists of expressions below for expressing and explaining preferences. If necessary, listen again to the people talking and fill in the gaps.

> **Phrase bank**
> **Expressing preferences**
> I .... listening to music.
> My .... thing of all is going to the theatre
> I .... being outdoors …
> Best of ...., I like gardening.
> I .... sports ....

50

Culture

> **Explaining preferences**
> What .... me .... is that …
> That's .... thing about …
> .... thing I .... gardening is that …
> And .... other .... is that I can …
> I can do it .... fun or ....
> I .... it relaxing.

Technique

Use different phrases to introduce preferences as these will provide variety and show you can use a range of language. Use *because* to explain why you prefer something.

3 With a partner, ask and answer the Speaking Part 1 questions below, using the expressions in the list above to help you.
   a How do you spend your weekends?
   b What else do you like doing in your free time?

Dealing with unfamiliar topics

1 Which of the activities below do you know something about? Which do you know little about?

   playing a musical instrument ■ painting ■ cookery

2 Match each question 1–4 with an answer a–d.
   1 Are you able to play any musical instruments?
   2 Do you have any artistic abilities?
   3 What sort of food do you enjoy cooking and eating?
   4 Which games do you enjoy playing?

   a I'm afraid I have absolutely no skill in this area at all. But I might learn in the future. It is simply too expensive to live on fast food.
   b I don't normally play games. When I was a child, I spent all my free time playing in the countryside, rather than playing proper games. And now I have little time for games – I relax by reading.
   c Unfortunately not. I have very little practical ability, and things like that are difficult for me. I tried when I was at school, but without success.
   d I wish I could. My parents made me take lessons when I was very young, but I just made a terrible noise and they let me give it up. I don't think I have any ability in that direction.

3 Answer these questions about the responses in exercise 2.
   a What do all four responses have in common?
   b Which expressions does each speaker use to say 'no'?
   c Match the answers (a, b, c, d) with the content in the table below. Some answers have more than one kind of content.

Content of answer	Answer
Past experience and the result	
No past experience and the reason	
A reference to future intentions and hopes	
A reference to personal level of skill	

Unit 6

4 With a partner, practise asking and answering these questions, which may be difficult for some candidates. Use the expressions you identified in exercise 3.

  a Are you interested in drawing?
  b Do you like singing?
  c Can you dance?
  d Are you good at making things?

5 With a partner, ask and answer this typical Speaking Part 1 question sequence.

  a Do you have any hobbies?
  b How and why did you first get involved in this activity?
  c Would you recommend it to another person? Why/Why not?

> **Technique**
> Say why it is difficult to answer – if it is difficult to answer. Say what experience you have of this kind of thing. Explain your personal situation. Talk about how you might like to do this kind of thing in future.

Pronunciation: shifting syllable stress

1 🔊 2.3 Listen and underline the stressed syllables in these words.

phi lo so phy   ge o gra pher   bi o lo gi cal

2 🔊 2.4 Complete the table and underline the stressed syllables. Then listen and check.

Subject	Person	Adjective
	geographer	
biology		
		philosophical

3 🔊 2.5 Add these words to the table in the correct places and mark the stress. The stress does not follow the exact pattern of the other words. Listen and check.

politics ■ politician ■ political ■ history ■ historian ■ historical

4 Fill in the gaps in this Speaking module Part 1 dialogue using the words in the box. Then practise the dialogue.

biology ■ psychology ■ biological ■ psychologists ■ psychology

Examiner: What are you studying now?
Candidate: I am studying **1** _____ at the moment but I am changing to **2** _____ sciences next year.
Examiner: Why is that?
Candidate: Too many people are studying **3** _____ now so there are not enough jobs for **4** _____ . **5** _____ is still expanding and so I hope there will be a job for me when I have finished.

> **Technique**
> Make sure you can pronounce the key words in the subject(s) that you are studying and that you might want to talk about in the Speaking module.

Exam listening

Section 3

🔊 2.6

Questions 21–26

Choose the correct letter **A**, **B** *or* **C**.

21 What is the main topic of the assignment?

  A the historical development of television
  B the development of new media
  C the cultural future of television

22 The main advantage of television is

  A its flexible schedules
  B its screen size
  C its shopping and social contacts

23 According to the tutor, the average length of a television programme might become

  A 45 minutes.
  B four to five minutes.
  C ten minutes.

24 What part of the library is going to be closed for one week?

  A the Sociology section
  B the Media Studies section
  C the Journals section

25 Which body do they decide to complain to?

  A the Premises Committee
  B the Students' Union
  C the library

26 What will the reprographics office do?

  A send emails to your tutor
  B send your dissertation to you
  C send your dissertation to your tutor

🔊 2.7

Questions 27–30

Write **NO MORE THAN THREE WORDS AND/OR A NUMBER** *for each answer.*

27 What is the big challenge for television and the Internet?

28 What is the title of Mrs Jones's lecture?

29 Where is the lecture?

30 When is the final date for the assignment?

7 Arts and sciences

UNIT AIMS

LISTENING SKILLS
Making questions from statements
Paraphrasing for matching

SPEAKING SKILLS
Comparing and evaluating
Expressing others' views
Pronunciation: weak forms and /ə/

Topic talk

1 Describe the two photos.

2 Answer the questions below.
   a Do you think that artists and scientists are born or are they made? Why/Why not?
   b What kind of attributes do you need to study sciences or the arts? Do scientists and artists both need to be creative?
   c Do you think it is possible for students to combine both the arts and sciences at school or university? Why/Why not?
   d What made you choose the subject(s) you are studying? If you could, would you change your mind now?

3 Decide which adjective best matches the descriptions a–i below.
   Example
   a ostentatious

   | original ■ talented ■ rigorous ■ curious ■ accomplished ostentatious ■ expressive ■ impartial ■ creative |

   a He's very pretentious and likes to show everyone how rich he is.
   b He plays the violin so well.
   c His approach to experiments is very precise and methodical.
   d She may be a budding artist but her work is very avant-garde and has never been seen before.
   e She has been described as a very gifted and ingenious sculptor.
   f His poems are very moving as they show his emotions clearly.
   g He has to be neutral in his work and cannot allow his emotions to take over.
   h His books are full of original ideas.
   i Even as a young chemist she had a very inquiring mind and investigated everything thoroughly.

4 Write the noun form for each adjective in exercise 3.
   Example
   ostentatious, *ostentation*

> **Technique**
> Keep a record of adjectives relating to people's personality and attributes. Record examples for the adjectives and write other words such as nouns related to the adjective, e.g. *creative/creativity*.

Arts and sciences

5 With a partner, choose five nouns or adjectives from exercises 3 and 4 and explain why the qualities are necessary. Give your own reasons.

Example
Why does an artist need to be talented/have talent?
Someone who is involved in the arts has to have talent, because …

6 In the IELTS Listening component, you may have to listen to someone talking about rules, procedures or guidelines. Look at the list below and decide what the speaker is talking about in a–h.

Example
And finally you have to have the report on the chemistry experiment in by the end of the week.
assignment deadline

- assignment deadline
- society/club constitution
- set of instructions
- assessment criteria
- application
- assignment guidelines
- examination rules and regulations
- hall of residence regulations

a You must be in by midnight, as the doors are locked. You must then call the porter.
b When the final bell rings, you must put your pens down immediately.
c The essay on Fine Art needs to be typed and bound.
d The use of PowerPoint is a must. Your physics experiment will be marked on your presentation.
e It is essential that members follow the rules at all times.
f All you need to know about how to do this is contained in this booklet.
g All history essays must be handed in by noon on Friday.
h When you send the form, two photographs need to be included.

7 Work with a partner and describe your reaction to one or more of the items in the list in exercise 6. For example, do you like trying to meet assignment deadlines?

8 Decide which of the following words mean the same as *compulsory*.

> not optional ■ mandatory ■ certain ■ obligatory ■ possible ■ requisite ■ vital ■ imperative ■ crucial

9 Work with a partner and give your own explanation for the questions below. In each case, use two of the following phrases in your answer: *in order to, because, for example, like* or *if*.
a Why is it necessary to present assignments well in all disciplines?
b What is the effect of visuals in a presentation? Do you think they should be compulsory even in essays?
c What is the benefit of a bibliography when you produce an essay?
d Why is preparation for any assignment crucial?
e Is writing a draft of an essay or report essential? Why/Why not?
f What in your opinion is the key to preparing a good assignment?
g What qualities do you need to show when you are making a presentation of your work?

Unit 7

Listening skills Making questions from statements

1 The questions below are taken from a multiple-choice task. Read questions 1–5 carefully and answer the questions below.

  a What is the general topic?
  b What group of people is the speaker talking to?

2 Some of the question stems are phrased as statements. Rephrase each statement as a question.

Example
Teachers visiting a festival should arrive at …
When should teachers visiting the festival arrive?

> **Technique**
> Pay attention to the stems (i.e. the first part) of multiple-choice questions. After that, look carefully and quickly at the alternatives and think about the relationship between the stem and the alternatives (e.g. cause and effect).

Questions 1–5

Choose the correct letter **A**, **B** *or* **C**.

1 What will the head of science probably do?

  A arrange the visit to the festival
  B confirm the school placements
  C provide information about the festival

2 The student teachers should arrange visits that last

  A one or two days.
  B two or three days.
  C all three days.

3 The most important purpose of festival visits is to

  A get better exam grades.
  B create enthusiasm for science.
  C enable students to have fun.

4 The central features of our scientific age are

  A inventions and improvements.
  B interesting and unusual events.
  C interest and enthusiasm for science.

5 What kind of specialists are teaching maths?

  A physicists
  B biologists
  C chemists

3 🔊 2.8 Listen to the recording and answer questions 1–5 in exercise 2.

Arts and sciences

Paraphrasing for matching

1 Read the extract below from a review of the book *Science in our World*. Match each chapter subject a–e with the chapter numbers 1–5.

> Chapter 1 concerns the purpose of science in the early days, namely to foretell the future by studying the stars. Science has had a long journey through the past centuries and this story is told in Chapter 2. The catastrophes that science has caused in the world are dealt with in Chapter 3. Some biographies of the celebrated names of science are given in Chapter 4. Finally, the innovations that science has brought to our lives are covered in Chapter 5.

Technique
Predict the words or phrases you might hear in matching tasks by thinking of synonyms or paraphrases for options given.

Science in our World

Contents

Chapter 1: _____   a *history* of science
Chapter 2: _____   b *famous* scientists
Chapter 3: _____   c *astrology* and science
Chapter 4: _____   d *new things* from science
Chapter 5: _____   e scientific *disasters*

2 Underline synonyms or paraphrases in the extract which match the words in italics in a–e above.

3 The questions below are taken from a matching task. Read the questions and options carefully. Then answer questions a–d below.

A	a show
B	an event of local interest
C	a technical demonstration
D	an open discussion
E	an interactive event
6	Waterworld ....
7	Transport 2050 ....
8	Science in a suitcase ....
9	Ropes and hangings ....
10	Paper and time ....

a What kinds of options are given in A–E?
b What do the capital letters in 6–10 tell you?
c Which list do you expect to be paraphrased in the recording?
d Which words or expressions might be used by the speakers to paraphrase this list? Make a list for each item.

4 🔊 2.9 Listen to the recording and answer the questions in exercise 3. Write the correct letters A–E next to the questions 6–10.

Unit 7

Speaking skills Comparing and evaluating

1 Read the short texts below and answer the questions.

> The sculptor made a laughing head. He put it on a stand and entered it for the modern art competition. The head became separated from the stand. This left the stand and a little stick of wood on the top. The judges never saw the head, but the stand and stick of wood was presented to them and they awarded it a prize. The sculptor was surprised but very happy.

> He was quickly cleaning up his laboratory and put an old dish of liquid on a window shelf. He locked up and went home. A few weeks later he remembered the dish and looked at it. Then he saw something unusual about the liquid. And so penicillin was born!

   a What was the accident that happened in each case? What was the result of each accident?
   b Which are more important – the accidents of science or the accidents of art?

2 Separate the words and phrases into two lists: words and phrases associated with the arts and those associated with the sciences.

   Arts _____
   Sciences _____

   > numeracy ■ knowledge of humanity ■ performance
   > analytical ■ creative ■ demonstration ■ discipline
   > mysterious ■ knowledge of the universe ■ experiment
   > certainty ■ literacy ■ incremental ■ work of art
   > imagination ■ original ■ definite ■ uncertainty

3 Answer these questions about the lists you made in exercise 2.
   a Which words were difficult to categorize?
   b Can you think of examples to justify applying some science words to the arts and vice versa?

4 Read the three typical Speaking Part 3 questions below. Which questions require a *comparison* in response? Which require an *evaluation*?
   a Which provides the best entertainment: a novel or a film?
   b To what extent have people's lives been improved by science?
   c To what degree are our lives improved by the arts?
   d Which is more important in modern cultures: scientific or artistic ability?

Arts and sciences

5 Phrases 1–6 below can be used to answer the questions in exercise 4. Match the phrases with the questions. One phrase can go with more than one question.
  1. The key difference between the two is …
  2. Oh, very much. For example, …
  3. Very little. The justification for these things is …
  4. They are both crucial for our daily lives, but of the two I would say …
  5. Making a choice between these two is very difficult because …
  6. I think … is more important because …

6 With a partner, ask and answer the questions in exercise 4. Use the phrases above in your answers.

> **Technique**
> Make sure you answer the question. For example, you may need to compare novels and films in general – a comparison. Or, you may need to give your opinion on quality – an evaluation. Don't just talk about the last film you saw.

Expressing others' views

1 Some students expressed these opinions about science and the arts. Read their statements and decide whether you agree or disagree. Change the opinions so that they express your views.

> Science has the ability to make all our lives much easier.

> The arts teach us what it means to be human.

> Most of the arts are of no practical use and are a waste of time.

> Science will certainly lead the world to disaster.

2 2.10 Listen to three speakers answer Speaking Part 3 questions. Match each speaker with the correct question a–c.

Speaker 1: _____

Speaker 2: _____

Speaker 3: _____

  a. To what extent should the arts be sponsored by government?
  b. Why do you think some people are distrustful of science?
  c. How can new technology help in our domestic lives?

3 Which one of these arguments does each speaker in exercise 2 agree with?
  a. Technology just creates more work.
  b. The arts contribute to society.
  c. Technology makes tasks easier.
  d. Scientists aren't engaged with the world.
  e. The arts should be more commercial.
  f. Scientists understand the impact of their ideas.

> **Technique**
> Use the following structure (to give yourself time to think): Give commonly held opinions first, comment on them and then give your own opinion. This is especially useful in Part 3.

4 2.10 Listen to the three speakers again. Check your answers to exercise 3 and complete the table below with the phrases each speaker uses to introduce other people's opinions.

5 2.10 Listen a final time. Make a note of the phrases the speakers use to disagree with other people's opinions.

Other people's opinions

Speaker 1: _____

Speaker 2: _____

Speaker 3: _____

Disagreeing

Speaker 1: _____

Speaker 2: _____

Speaker 3: _____

59

Unit 7

6 With a partner, ask and answer the Speaking Part 3 question sequences below. Use the phrases in exercises 3 and 4 to introduce other views and your own.

Sequence 1
a What harm can science do to us?
b Which is more important in our society today, the sciences or the arts?
c Should governments subsidize scientific research? Why?

Sequence 2
a How big a part do machines play in our lives today?
b What are some of the problems with being so dependent on machines?
c To what extent would it be better to lead a simpler life, without advanced technology?

Pronunciation: weak forms and /ə/

1 2.11 Each of these words has the sound /ə/ in it once. Listen and underline the /ə/ sound. You will hear the /ə/ sound first.

about ■ Internet ■ doctor

2 2.12 Look at the words in **bold** in the following sentences. In one case the word is pronounced with /ə/, in one case it is not. Listen and underline the word which has /ə/.
a The city of Northbridge has **some** ultra-modern buildings, **some** of which are in the science park.
b **There** is a university **there**, also.
c **That** makes it the most important science park **that** you will find in this part of the country.

3 Put a tick (✓) or a cross (✗), as appropriate in the table.

	/ə/ used for the vowel sound ✓/✗
Some meaning a part of a greater number	
Some meaning an indefinite amount	
There meaning a place	
There introducing a sentence	
That pointing at something	
That connecting two parts of a sentence	

4 2.13 Underline the words in bold below which are pronounced with /ə/. Listen and check your answers.

The Mercury Gallery has opened an art exhibition in Bond Street. **There** are paintings by foreign and British artists **there**. You can see **some** examples of the best **that** modern art can offer. **Some** works are abstract and **some** are figurative, but all are wonderfully imaginative. **That** is why the exhibition is so popular.

5 Practise saying the text, pronouncing the /ə/ in the right places.

Arts and sciences

Exam listening

Section 3

🔊 2.14

Questions 21–25

Complete the notes below.

Write **NO MORE THAN THREE WORDS AND/OR A NUMBER** for each answer.

The Arts Association receives **21** $ .... million from the government.

The first issue the Arts Association tries to address is **22** ....

All the issues mean that the arts are for **23** ....

The government wants **24** .... in return for its contribution.

The **25** .... programme helps organizations with financial problems.

🔊 2.15

Questions 26–30

What is the subject of each of the books Mr Simpson recommended to Arthur?

Choose your answers from the list and write the letters **A–F** next to the question numbers.

A financial information
B psychology of art
C art and other media
D modern art
E history of art
F the art market

Greenberg   **26** ....
Parliamentary report **27** ....
Dennison   **28** ....
Hampton   **29** ....
Frick   **30** ....

8 Nature

UNIT AIMS

LISTENING SKILLS
Changing opinions
Answering multiple-choice questions
Completing a summary (2)

SPEAKING SKILLS
Describing animals
Describing presents
Pronunciation: contrastive stress

Topic talk

1 Describe the photo and answer questions a–d.

   a Do you find places like the scene in the picture beautiful or boring?
   b Why are places like this attractive to people?
   c Why do we need places like this more and more in the modern world?
   d What kind of places do you like to visit? Do you prefer places in towns and cities or in the countryside?

2 Decide whether the statements below show the speaker is enthusiastic or unenthusiastic about a place.

   a The holiday cottage caught my attention immediately, so I bought it.
   b I have been fascinated by the building since I first saw it.
   c As it's in the middle of nowhere, it's very peaceful.
   d The house is basically okay.
   e Living in such a remote area is just about bearable.
   f Even though it's in the middle of the city, it's not at all noisy.
   g What makes the place so attractive is the open fields.
   h The reason why it appeals to me is the sound of the crashing waves at night.

3 Add the following phrases to as many of the sentences a–h above as you can.

   Example
   a 2;5

   1 but it's in danger of being spoilt by tourists visiting it.
   2 but sadly I haven't visited it for years.
   3 In fact, at times it's quieter than the countryside.
   4 but I'm afraid that won't last long.
   5 but at times it can be lonely there.

Nature

4 Read the example below. Then rewrite sentences a–g, beginning with *what*.

Example
The open fields make the place so attractive.
What makes the place so attractive is the open fields.

  a The silence there makes me feel so relaxed.

  b Being away from the city does me a lot of good.

  c The place is restful because there are no shops.

  d The sea is clean because there are no factories.

  e The trees make the garden very private.

  f The people make the area so welcoming.

  g The area is appealing because it has many tourist attractions.

Technique
Use different structures in the speaking component to add variety, such as *The house is quiet because there are no neighbours. What makes the house quiet is not having (any) neighbours.* Learn to recognize information expressed in different ways in the listening component as well.

5 With a partner, practise asking questions beginning with *why* based on the statements in exercise 4. Then answer with sentences beginning with *what*.

Example
Why is the place so relaxing?
What makes me relaxed there is the silence.

6 In Speaking Part 2, you may be asked to talk about a place or something else from your personal experience. Complete each of the statements below with an example from your own life.

  a The building that I like most is …

  b The pet I remember best is …

  c The present I will never forget was …

  d The incident that embarrassed me most was …

  e One holiday I will never forget was …

  f A school trip I remember well was …

Technique
Notice how different types of structures are repeated in parts of the exam. For example, in Speaking Part 2 you usually begin with a noun phrase with a defining relative clause, e.g. *The building that I like most is …*

7 Write a follow-up sentence with *what* to develop each of the ideas in exercise 6.

Example
What I like most about the building is the large windows.

8 With a partner, describe the items and experiences in exercise 6. Start with your sentences. Then develop your ideas using the words below.

  because ▪ as ▪ since ▪ with ▪ which

63

Unit 8

Listening skills Changing opinions

1 Read the four dialogues below.
  a Which speakers change their minds?
  b What phrases do they use to indicate this?

1
A What river's that?
B That's the River Exe, no, I mean the River Avon.

2
C Ben Nevis is the tallest mountain in Scotland. In the UK, in fact.
D Really?

3
E If we leave now, we will see the sunset.
F I'm not so sure about that. The sky looks very cloudy.
E Actually, you're right. It might be better to wait until another day.

4
G If we visit the lake this afternoon, we may see the ducks flying in.
H I think you'll find they come in greater numbers in the evening.
G Yes, that's what I meant, in the evening. We'll see thousands in the evening.

2 Read the dialogue. Then answer questions a–c below.

Boy	What shall we do this morning? We can visit the monkeys first – they're always fun.
Girl	But the monkeys will be fed in the afternoon. That will be the best time to see them.
Boy	Well, we can see the elephants, then.
Girl	The keepers bring them out after midday too.
Boy	Then we should visit the aquarium – the fish are always awake.
Girl	That's a good idea. We'll see the fish. And what about the lions?
Boy	The big cat enclosure is not open today, although we can see the tigers this morning if we want.
Girl	Yes, let's see those and the fish. And then we can have lunch.
Boy	All right. Let's go.

Technique
Listen carefully for speakers who change their opinion. In extended multiple-choice questions, you may hear most or all of the options on the recording. When speakers change their minds, you cannot answer the question with certainty until the discussion is finished.

  a How many animals do they talk about visiting?
  b How many animals do they decide to visit?
  c At what stage in the conversation do you know their decision: the beginning, the middle or the end?

Answering multiple-choice questions

1 The questions in exercise 3 on page 65 come from an extended multiple-choice task. Skim read the questions. Which of the following topics do you think you will hear about? Which are not so likely? Put a tick (✓), question mark (?) or a cross (✗) by each one.

animals ■ assignments ■ circuses ■ zoos ■ television
schools ■ car accidents ■ banks ■ museums

Technique
Skim read the questions and the alternatives to get the idea of what the recording will be about. This will help you to understand it better.

64

Nature

2 Now think about the topic of the listening text, by answering these questions.

What is the difference between:
- a zoo and a circus?
- predator and prey?
- entertainment and education?
- a cage and a park?
- wild and domestic?
- conservation and extinction?

Technique
Spend a little time thinking about the topic before you listen to the recording. Ask yourself: *What do I know about this subject already?*

3

Questions 1–3

Choose THREE letters **A–G**.

What topics must the assignment cover?

- **A** zoo finances
- **B** public safety
- **C** the history of zoos
- **D** animal welfare
- **E** education and zoos
- **F** zoos for science
- **G** value for money

Questions 4 and 5

Choose TWO letters **A–E**.

Which areas do the students decide to concentrate their efforts on?

- **A** science
- **B** history
- **C** entertainment
- **D** conservation
- **E** education

Technique
Put the answers in any order, e.g. A, C or C, A, etc.

4 🔊 2.16 Listen to the first part of the recording and answer questions 1–5.

Completing a summary (2)

1 The paragraph below is taken from a summary completion task. Read the paragraph and decide what kind of information is missing in each question. Match each space 6–10 with a phrase from the list.

> an activity ■ a person ■ a date ■ a number ■ a place ■ a colour ■ an adjective

> The Arabian oryx is mainly **6** _____ in colour. It lives in a **7** _____ climate. In **8** _____ it became extinct. Now, there are about **9** _____ in Oman. A crash in the population was caused by **10** _____ .

2 🔊 2.17 Listen to the second part of the recording and complete the summary. Write NO MORE THAN TWO WORDS AND/OR A NUMBER for each answer.

65

Unit 8

Speaking skills Describing animals

1 Read the short texts in which people talk about pets they had as children. Match each description a–c with an animal from the list.

cat ■ parrot ■ dog ■ rabbit ■ horse ■ goldfish ■ mouse

a
We had him for about ten years. I grew up with him, I suppose. He was always very lively when someone new arrived at the house, jumping up and wagging his tail. The fondest memory I have is of taking him for walks along the canal. I also enjoyed throwing a stick for him in the park. When he was happy he'd bark a lot. I really miss him.

b
She was a real character. I wouldn't say she was friendly – quite the opposite, in fact. She had a habit of arching her back and scratching people she didn't like. But what I remember most is letting her curl up on my lap, and then stroking her. I'm not sure who found it the most relaxing, me or her. She certainly liked it, and she always purred very loudly.

c
Looking after her involved quite a lot of work. We used to have to go to the farm every night with a bale of hay to feed her. I also used to groom her, which was fun, but hard work. So it was all quite tough, but worth it in the end. What sticks in my mind is the way she used to get excited just before we started jumping. They were very happy times.

> **Technique**
> Prepare some vocabulary relating to animals and pets. Then you will be able to answer questions on this topic in Parts 1 and 2.

2 Read the descriptions again. Complete the first column of the table below with the name of the animal. Then write verbs typical of that animal in the second column. One has been done for you.

Animal	Typical actions	Human actions
a _____	*jump up*	_____
b _____	_____	_____
c _____	_____	_____

3 Complete the third column with verbs that describe what people typically do with these animals, for example *take them for walks*.

4 Each text in exercise 1 contains a phrase for introducing a memory. Find and underline these three phrases.

5 🔊 2.18 Listen to three people talking about animals and pets. Decide which speaker is answering which question below.
   a What was your pet like?
   b Have you ever had a favourite pet?
   c What was your favourite pet animal when you were a child?

66

Nature

6 🔊 **2.18** Listen again. What phrase does each speaker use to show he/she does not regard the animal as a pet?

Speaker 1: … although _____ a pet, _____ .

Speaker 2: I'm _____ is a real pet …

Speaker 3: _____ , he wasn't my pet at all …

7 The task card below is taken from Speaking Part 2. Take one minute to think and make notes about your own talk on this topic, using your own experience. Then practise speaking for two minutes using your notes.

> Describe an animal which belonged to you or someone you know.
>
> You should say
>
> what type of animal it was
>
> what personality it had
>
> what it typically did
>
> and explain your own personal reaction to the animal.

Describing presents

1 Read the following slogan from a public information campaign. Then answer questions a–c below.

> A pet is for life.

a What do you think the campaign is about?
b Do you think animals make good gifts?
c What questions should you ask yourself before you give a gift like this?

2 The list below gives common occasions on which people give presents. Answer questions a–c below.

> wedding ▪ birthday ▪ wedding anniversary ▪ religious festival
> moving house ▪ leaving a job ▪ visiting a friend's home

a On which of these occasions do you give presents in your country?
b Are there any other occasions on which you give presents?
c What presents are suitable for each occasion?

Technique
Prepare vocabulary relating to cultural activities, e.g. festivities and holidays, including any food or drink associated with them.

3 Read these two articles about present giving. Then answer questions a–c below.

Present madness

The greetings card industry is making more and more money every year. There are so many occasions on which we must give greetings cards now. Mother's Day and Father's Day require cards and presents from all to all. Soon, I firmly believe, we will have Brother's, Sister's, Uncle's, Aunt's, and probably Dog's Days. All needing a card, all needing a present. Someone, please, say 'Enough!'.

East meets west

We are picking up the delightful habits of some Asian countries. Small, carefully and tastefully wrapped presents for all kinds of informal occasions – and sometimes for no occasion at all – are the fashion among young people everywhere now. A wonderful fashion it is, too.

a Which article is critical of present and card giving?
b Do you enjoy giving cards and presents? Do you like receiving them?
c Should we give and receive presents more frequently than we do?

Unit 8

4 Read this Speaking Part 2 task card. Take a minute to think and make notes about your own talk on this topic, using your own experience. Then practise speaking for two minutes using your notes.

> Describe a present you received and that you liked very much.
>
> You should say
>
> who gave the present to you and on what occasion
>
> what it was like
>
> what you did with it
>
> and explain why you liked the present.

Technique

Think of an object which you did something active with, or which you received on a special occasion so you'll have something to say.

Pronunciation: contrastive stress

1 🔊 2.19 Underline the main or sentence stress in the following sentences. The first one has been done for you. Listen and check.

   a We had a problem with security.
      We had a problem with sec<u>ur</u>ity.
   b We wanted an active dog.
   c We wanted him to bark at intruders.
   d We wanted him to bite burglars.
   e We wanted him to wake up at the sound of the alarm.

2 Delete as appropriate to state the rule:

The main or sentence stress is normally on the *first/last* content word in the sentence.

3 🔊 2.20 Extra parts (in *italics*) have been added to four of the sentences in exercise 1. Listen to the longer sentences and underline the main stress in each part of the sentence. The first one has been done for you.

   a We wanted an <u>a</u>ctive dog, *but we got a <u>la</u>zy dog.*
   b We wanted him to bark at intruders, *but he licked intruders.*
   c We wanted him to bite burglars, *but he welcomed burglars.*
   d We wanted him to wake up at the sound of the alarm, *but he fell asleep at the sound of it.*

4 Delete as appropriate to state the rule:

When there is a contrast of ideas, *the contrasting words/the repeated words* carry the main stress.

5 Now say the sentences in exercise 3, putting the stress in the same places as in the recording.

6 🔊 2.21 A candidate is describing, in Speaking Part 2, a product he bought which was not satisfactory. He chose to speak about a bicycle.

   a In the phrases in **bold**, underline a suitable word to carry the main stress.
      … firstly, the bell. It is one thing **to have a quiet bell**, but this **was a whispering bell**. Then the light: at night one **needs a bright light**, not like this one, which was **the faintest of lights**. Then, it was heavy. I needed to take it on the train, so **a light bike was what I needed**. I sold it back to the shop and **bought a more expensive bike**, which I still have – **my dream bike**. But **while I had the bike** …
   b Listen and check.
   c Say the candidate's words, using the appropriate stress.

Exam listening

Section 4

🔊 2.22

Questions 31–33

Choose **THREE** letters, A–G

Which **THREE** features of the starling does the lecturer talk about?

A   nesting
B   longevity
C   feeding
D   mating
E   bringing up young
F   global distribution
G   parental roles

Questions 34–37

Compete the summary below

Write **ONE WORD ONLY** for each answer

> **Problems with starlings**
>
> Thousands of birds can congregate and feed on commercial **34** ....
>
> The farmers suffer great **35** .... damage and the public have to tolerate the **36** ....
>
> It is suspected that the birds carry **37** .... which can be harmful to humans.

Questions 38–40

Choose the correct letter **A, B** or **C**.

38 What is the best of the three approaches?

   A   limitation
   B   legislation
   C   prevention

39 What is regulated by legislation on species movements?

   A   the movement of foreigners
   B   the deposit and pick-up of water
   C   the import and export of fish

40 What is the ultimate deciding factor in species management?

   A   economics
   B   ethics
   C   politics

9 Health

UNIT AIMS

LISTENING SKILLS
Predicting in tables (2)
Spelling words

SPEAKING SKILLS
Recognizing similar questions
Emphasizing main points
Taking time to think
Pronunciation: using two intonation patterns

Topic talk

1 Look at the photos and answer questions a–d below.

a Which of these sports would you like to play? Which would you prefer to watch?
b Which of these sports are most and least beneficial to your health?
c Which sports are the most popular in your country? Why?
d Which categories below do the sports in the photos belong to? Think of other sports for each category.

water sports ■ adventure sports ■ motor sports ■ blood sports
team sports ■ non-contact sports ■ racket sports ■ indoor sports
outdoor sports

2 Match each statement 1–6 with the correct explanation a–f.

1 I prefer contact sports like football and rugby,
2 Swimming is the only individual sport I like,
3 Everyone should take up some form of physical exercise,
4 I like skiing and other winter sports,
5 I suppose I'm mostly interested in spectator sports,
6 The kinds of sports I'm really against are blood sports,

a since it will keep them healthy and prevent illness.
b basically because I'm not a very energetic person.
c just because I don't believe people should take pleasure in that sort of thing.
d not least because they're a good way to get rid of my aggression.
e but they're obviously difficult to do all year round.
f as I usually prefer being with other people.

Technique

Support main points and ideas with explanations which contain reasons, examples or doubts/reservations.

Health

3 With a partner, ask and answer these questions. Give reasons for your answers.
   a What is your favourite sport?
   b Which areas of sport appeal to you?
   c Which areas of sport would you avoid?

4 Decide which two words in the list cannot follow the word *sport*s.

> event ■ opponent ■ centre ■ club ■ field ■ opportunity ■ venue
> coverage ■ equipment ■ channel

5 The personal statements below were made by people who enjoy sport. Make the statements more abstract.

Example
Doing sport has made me more mentally alert. → *Doing sport makes people more mentally alert.*

   a Since I've been doing more exercise, I get fewer illnesses.
   b One thing that's important is that I'm still learning new skills.
   c Part of the reason I play football is to meet new people.
   d After doing some exercise, I always feel more relaxed.
   e Something you have to learn is how to be part of a team.
   f The main reason I take part is because there's a competitive atmosphere.
   g I was partly attracted to do more sport by the opportunity to be outdoors.

6 State a general benefit for each statement in exercise 5. Which three statements do you think are the most important?

7 In Speaking Part 3, you will be asked to respond to some more abstract questions. Match the benefits you identified in exercise 6 with the questions below.
   a What do you think is the link between sport and a healthy population?
   b What do you think is the cause of the increase in people doing sport?
   c How important is the social aspect of participating in sport?

8 With a partner, ask and answer the questions in exercise 7. Give more detailed examples, using the phrases in exercise 5 and the trigger words below to help you.

> if ... , then ■ for example ■ so ■ that ■ as ■ because ■ since

Technique
Visualize what you are talking about if you can.

Unit 9

Listening skills Predicting in tables (2)

1 The list below contains some problems which students often encounter at university. Number them from 1–6 according to how serious you think they are (1 = the most serious; 6 = the least serious).

feeling homesick

examination pressure

colds and flu

poor accommodation

language difficulties

student debt

2 Answer questions a–c below.
  a Which other problems can new students encounter?
  b Look at the table in exercise 3 below. Which of the student services listed could help with the problems mentioned in exercise 1?
  c If you experienced problems at university, who would you go to for help?

3 The table below comes from a table completion task. Answer questions a–c.
  a What do the numbers tell you about the order in which you will hear the information?
  b Which of the missing spaces are likely to be numbers? What kind of numbers?
  c What can you predict for the other gaps?

Staying healthy at Glenfield

Student services	Location	Cost	Availability
Health centre	North Campus	Example: ....£6.50.... charge for prescriptions	All students within the **1** .... zone
Counselling service	North Campus	Up to **2** .... consultations free	All students
Nightline	**3** .... Campus	Free	By phone: call **4** ....
Sports centre	South Campus	**5** £............... each year	All students

4 🔊 2.23 Listen to the recording and complete the table. Write ONE WORD AND/OR A NUMBER for each answer.

72

Health

Spelling words

1 Some letters in the English alphabet sound alike. For example *p* rhymes with *g*, and *a* rhymes with *j*. Complete the lists below with the remaining letters of the alphabet which rhyme with the first one.

a b c d e f g h i j k l m n o p q r s t u v w x y z

List 1: a, … … …
List 2: b, … … … … … … …
List 3: f, … … … … … …
List 4: i, …
List 5: q … …
List 6: r, o, (Neither of these rhymes with any other letters.)

2 🔊 **2.24** Listen to the lists you made in exercise 1 and check they are correct.

3 🔊 **2.25** Listen to a person leaving a message on an answering machine. Complete the form below.

> **Telephone message**
>
> Message for: ……………………………………………
>
> Message: ……………………………………………
>
> Caller's number: ……………………………………………
>
> Message from: ……………………………………………
>
> Time: …………………… Date: ……………………

Technique
Prepare for form-filling questions in Sections 1 and 2 by familiarizing yourself with the sounds in the English alphabet.

4 Make notes for a telephone message of your own, following the form above. With a partner, leave a message. Spell out words where necessary.

5 🔊 **2.26** Listen to the second part of the recording, which follows on from the table completion task in exercise 3 on page 72. Complete the form below. Write NO MORE THAN THREE WORDS AND/OR A NUMBER for each answer.

> **Material request form**
>
> Documents requested: **6** …………………………
>
> Student name: **7** …………………………
>
> Address: 22 **8** …………………………
>   Glenfield
>
> Postcode: **9** ………………… 9BQ
>
> Nationality: Dutch
>
> Age: 24
>
> Course: **10** ………………… and …………………

Unit 9

Speaking skills Recognizing similar questions

1 Read the ten ideas below on how to improve your health, and answer questions a–c.
  a How many of the ideas do you personally apply in your life?
  b Are there any ideas which you do not agree with?
  c Are there any other causes of poor health that the advice does not cover?

Ten easy ways to improve your health

  1 Apply sun cream when outdoors on sunny days.
  2 Eat at least five portions of fruit and vegetables each day.
  3 Stop smoking.
  4 Avoid high-fat convenience foods.
  5 Control how much salt and sugar you eat.
  6 Drink at least 1.5 litres of water each day.
  7 Start a holistic form of exercise, like yoga or tai chi.
  8 Take vitamin supplement tablets each day.
  9 Avoid stress by balancing work and play.
  10 Do thirty minutes of moderate exercise on most days.

2 In Speaking Part 3 you will be asked some abstract questions about a topic. It is important to be able to understand exactly what the examiner asks so that you can answer appropriately. Which questions below would have basically the same information in the answer?

Example
a is similar to g

  a In what ways is the modern diet better or worse than the diet of the past?
  b What are the main causes of ill-health in the modern world?
  c How can people take steps to improve their general level of health?
  d In what ways are sport and health linked?
  e Which factors are contributing to low levels of health in the world today?
  f Are sport and health connected? If so, how?
  g How is the food we eat different from the food eaten by previous generations?
  h To what extent can alternative approaches to medicine have a positive effect?
  i How effective is alternative medicine in helping people improve their health?
  j What are the most effective ways of getting and staying healthy?

3 Which ideas in exercise 1 are relevant to each question in exercise 2?

74

Health

Emphasizing main points

1 🔊 2.27 Listen to three speakers answering questions from exercise 2 on the previous page. Match each speaker with the correct question.

Speaker 1: _____

Speaker 2: _____

Speaker 3: _____

2 🔊 2.27 The list below gives some phrases for emphasizing your main points. Listen again to the three speakers. Match each phrase with the correct speaker.

It's mostly because of …
I suppose the best way is …
The main cause seems to be …
I'd say … is the key thing.
I suppose the most effective way is …
It's obvious that …

> **Technique**
> Use phrases like the ones in exercise 2 when you are sure of your opinion.

Taking time to think

1 The comments in a–c below were made to students preparing for Speaking Part 3. Which statement gives an accurate reflection of the test?
   a If you do not have a clear answer for every topic presented, you will get a bad mark.
   b If you do not have a clear answer to an unexpected question, you can admit this and give the best answer that you can.
   c If you do not have a clear answer to an unexpected question, you should tell the examiner and ask to move on to the next question.

2 🔊 2.27 Each speaker in the recording used a phrase to delay giving their answer. Listen again and write the phrases below.

Speaker 1: _____

Speaker 2: _____

Speaker 3: _____

3 With a partner, ask and answer the questions in exercise 2. Use the phrases for taking time to think and for emphasizing main points to help you express your own ideas. Give reasons for your answers.

> **Technique**
> Some questions may be difficult and unexpected. Take a moment to collect your thoughts and explain to the examiner that you are unsure. This will give you time to think though your score may be affected if you hesitate for too long.

Unit 9

4 Read the two short articles below and answer the questions.
  a In what ways do they disagree with the health advice we normally receive?
  b How would these articles change your answers to the questions you discussed in exercise 2 in the previous section?

Are you an exercise addict?
An occasional trip to the gym is fine, but increasing numbers of people find that exercise becomes the main organizing principle for each day. In extreme cases, some individuals have found that their exercise regime affects their job and their relationships. Nowadays everyone is very keen on healthy living, and this may become an even bigger problem in future.

An egg a day keeps the doctor away
Only a few years ago, we were being warned that there was so much cholesterol in eggs that we shouldn't eat more than two or three a week. Recently, nutritionists have changed their minds: eggs are no longer a danger food, and the cholesterol they contain has little or no effect on our health. Now we need to ask ourselves if we should really pay attention to the media about these matters.

5 With a partner, ask and answer the questions below.
  a How is good health related to education and wealth?
  b What dangers are associated with exercise and sport?
  c Is it possible to eat healthy food that is also enjoyable?

Pronunciation: using two intonation patterns

1 2.28 Listen to the five words. Enter the intonation pattern in the box.
  ↘ for *fall* intonation
  ↘↗ for *fall-rise* intonation

nine   bee   diet   question   answer
□   □   □   □   □

2 2.29 Listen to this part of a telephone number.
  347
What is the intonation pattern of the numbers: fall-rise or fall?

Listen to this complete telephone number:
  347 321
What is the intonation pattern of each group of numbers: fall-rise or fall?

3 Delete as appropriate to make the rule.
  a We can show that we have not finished a list by using the *fall-rise/fall* intonation.
  b We can show that we have finished a list by using the *fall-rise/fall* intonation.

4 2.30 Listen to these lists. The speakers have left some of these lists *unfinished* (i.e. ending with a *fall-rise* intonation); some are finished (ending with a *fall* intonation). Listen and select the right alternative; U is unfinished, F is finished.
  a 0797 543679   U/F
  b 0788 3421083   U/F
  c licence number 13DAK45   U/F
  d licence number 67SMI67   U/F
  e J-O-H-N   U/F
  f J-O-H-N-S   U/F
  g J-O-H-N-S-O-N   U/F

5 Say all the examples in exercise 4 in a way which shows they are finished.

Health

Exam listening

Section 2

🔊 2.31

Questions 11–15

Label the plan below.

*Write **NO MORE THAN TWO WORDS** for each answer.*

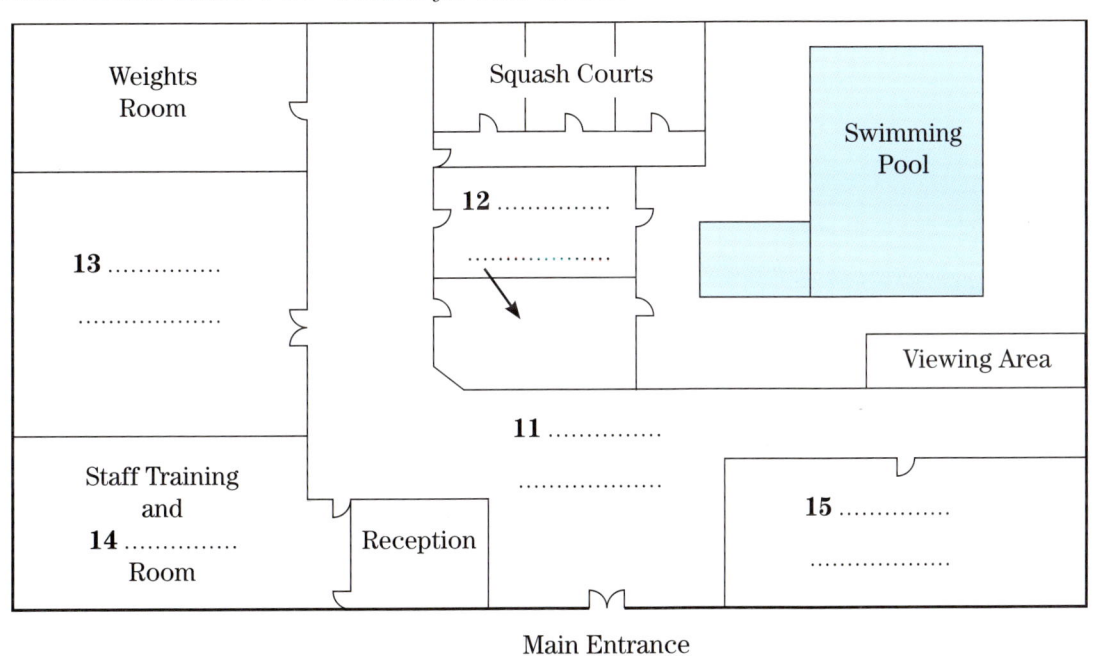

```
Weights Room        Squash Courts        Swimming Pool

                         12 ..............
13 ..............
   ..............
                                               Viewing Area

                    11 ..............
Staff Training
and                                     15 ..............
14 ..............   Reception
Room
                    Main Entrance
```

🔊 2.32

Questions 16–20

Complete the table below.

*Write **NO MORE THAN THREE WORDS OR A NUMBER** for each answer.*

Membership type	Cost	Access	Additional benefits
Anytime	**16** £	Anytime between 5 a.m. and midnight	Access to **17** .... clubs nationwide
Freetime	£500	Between 10 a.m. and 3 p.m.	Access to **18** ....
Standard	£400	Same as Freetime, but only **19**	None
Children	**20** .... % discount	Depends on choice of scheme	Depends on choice of scheme

77

10 The individual and society

UNIT AIMS

LISTENING SKILLS
Paraphrasing questions
Answering visual multiple-choice questions

SPEAKING SKILLS
Describing places and feelings
Starting your description
Summing up impressions
Pronunciation: using intonation in continuous speech

Topic talk

1 Look at the photo opposite and answer questions a–c.
  a How would you feel about being part of a crowd like this?
  b Do you think individuals shape society or is it the other way round? Why?
  c In what ways can people have a positive influence on the society they live in?

2 Complete sentences a–h below by adding an appropriate noun from the list. The first one has been done for you.

> issue ■ initiatives ■ difficulty ■ attitudes ■ aspect
> area ■ outline ■ alternative

  a Let's now examine the range of *initiatives* the government has introduced to promote social awareness.
  b Another major _____ that we face here is the quality of research.
  c One _____ of the problem that has yet to be considered is the cost to society.
  d Another problem _____ we must examine is the meaning of the word *society*.
  e Let us now look at the burning _____ of individual responsibility.
  f Let's start with a brief _____ of the course.
  g One obvious _____ to consider was closing the project down.
  h First, let us consider the various _____ people hold towards enterprise in society.

3 When you listen to a talk, you need to be able to follow the guidance given by the speaker. Decide the function of each of the sentences a–h above. Choose from the functions in 1–3 below.

Example
a 3

  1 the very beginning of a talk
  2 part of a sequence of points
  3 beginning a new sequence of points

The individual and society

4 Replace the words in the sentences in exercise 2 with words from the list below. In some cases, more than one word will be possible.

> question ■ sketch ■ summary ■ problem ■ viewpoints ■ hurdle
> proposals ■ obstacle ■ facet ■ plan

5 The extract below comes from a lecturer's talk. Decide which words in the extract can be replaced by the items a–g. Some words in the extract will be used more than once.

> **a** theories **b** requirement **c** need **d** topics
> **e** influence **f** effect **g** concerns

> In today's session, we are going to examine the latest thinking regarding the necessity for societies in the world to foster international cooperation on a wide range of issues. We are going to look into the dynamics of collaboration at a society level first and then see if individual organizations or indeed individuals can have any impact. So, let us now go through this list of problems on the first slide.

6 Match at least one solution from the list below to each international problem a–g.

> flood prevention ■ trade and political partnerships ■ investing strategically in job creation
> sharing information and technology ■ international water preservation programme
> sharing ideas on how to cope with changes ■ research into management of assets

- **a** Water shortages are a major cause for concern.
- **b** Some countries are too small to be heard on the international stage.
- **c** Poverty is increasing not declining.
- **d** Flooding is causing serious damage in both rich and poor countries.
- **e** Demographic changes are affecting the balance within societies.
- **f** Natural resources are becoming exhausted.
- **g** Some countries are being left behind while other countries are advancing rapidly.

7 With a partner, practise asking and answering the questions below. Use the ideas in exercise 6 to help you.
- **a** How do you think individuals can best contribute to society?
- **b** Do you think modern societies are in danger of being destroyed by materialism?
- **c** What is the impact of modern business developments worldwide on societies in general?

Unit 10

Listening skills Paraphrasing questions

1 For each statement below, decide whether it reflects your attitude to life.

   a I always wear exactly what I like. I don't care if other people think it's not fashionable.
   b Being on time is really important. It's important to respect others' feelings by not being late.
   c Is it always wrong to break the law? It depends. For small things it's OK, provided you don't get caught.
   d I normally do what the boss tells me at work. Even if I disagree, I keep my head down. It's easier that way.

2 Answer the questions below.

   a Would you describe yourself as a conformist or a rebel?
   b Which group makes the biggest contribution to society: conformists or rebels?

3 The questions below are taken from a short-answer question task. Sentences a and b come from Section 4 in the Listening module. Read the questions and decide which question sentences a and b relate to.

> **1** Where was Solomon Asch born?
> **2** Which area of interest made Asch take up psychology?
> **3** What was the name of Asch's famous experiment?
> **4** Who were the majority of participants in each experiment?
>
> **a** Asch was attracted to take up psychology because he was interested in ....
> **b** It was his interest in .... that made Asch decide to take up psychology.

Technique
Paraphrase questions in your head like this. It will help you to find possible answers.

4 For the other questions in exercise 3, write two gapped sentences that paraphrase the question.

5 🔊 2.33 Listen to the first part of the recording. Answer the questions 1–4 in exercise 3. Write NO MORE THAN THREE WORDS for each answer.

Answering visual multiple-choice questions

1 Look at question 5 (exercise 3) on the next page. Which pie chart in 5 is described by the sentence below?

   The pie chart shows that 15 per cent of people gave the right answer, whereas 85 per cent gave the wrong answer.

2 Write brief sentences describing pie charts A and C in question 5.

The individual and society

3 Write brief sentences describing the diagrams in question 6 below. Choose words from the list below to help you.

> equal ■ vertical ■ shortest ■ on the right ■ in the middle ■ longest ■ on the left ■ horizontal

Question 5

Which pie chart shows the proportion of people who gave the incorrect judgement?

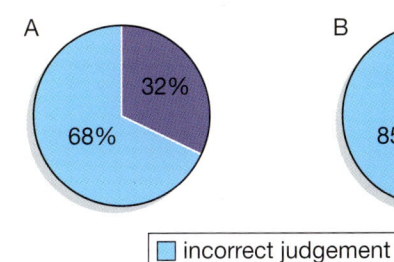

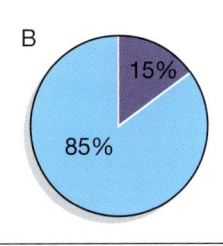

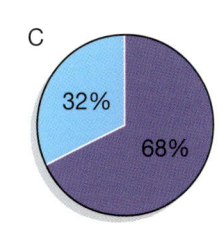

A B C

32% / 68%   15% / 85%   32% / 68%

□ incorrect judgement   □ correct judgement

Question 6

Which diagram shows the content of the first card used in the experiment?

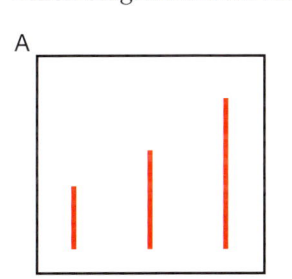

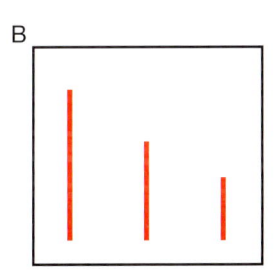

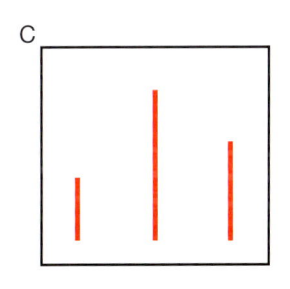

A   B   C

Technique
Predict the form of possible answers by paraphrasing what you see in the question.

4 🔊 2.34 Listen to the recording and answer questions 5 and 6 above and multiple-choice Questions 7–10 below.

Questions 7 and 8

Choose TWO letters **A–E**.

Which two features changed the results of the experiment?

A a bigger group

B the number of lines

C more time

D gender

E privacy

Questions 9 and 10

Choose TWO letters **A–E**.

What reasons did subjects give for conforming to the judgement of others?

A keep the experimenter happy

B give a good impression

C leave early

D please the other participants

E appear clever

Technique
Put the answers in any order, e.g. B, C or C, B.

Unit 10

Speaking skills Describing places and feelings

1 Read the texts below. What kind of place is being described in each text?

> There's something about the place that just feels oppressive. When I've finished what I have to do, I just want to get out as quickly as I can. I think it might be because of the fluorescent lighting, which gives me a bit of a headache, and the air-conditioning, which drones on and on. After I've been there all week, staring at those grey walls, I feel emotionally drained. But, that's life.

> It's difficult to describe what really invigorates me, just a freshness that feels good. I always go whenever I feel depressed about something and need a bit of cheering up. I love the sound of the water, which always relaxes me, and the saltiness in the air. There aren't normally many people around either. It's off the beaten track, so I always manage to get the place more or less to myself.

2 Answer the questions below about places and feelings.
   a What types of place attract you? Which do you avoid? Why?
   b In what ways can places affect our sense of well-being?
   c How do the places we grow up in affect our character?

3 Complete the sentences below with adjectives from the list. What places do you think these are?

> dull ■ busy ■ deserted ■ exciting ■ peaceful ■ wild ■ colourful ■ friendly

   a I like it because it's so _____ . It's nice to be where there are lots of people.
   b I suppose it's quite a _____ place. There isn't much of interest to do.
   c Sometimes it's completely _____ . There's nobody around at all.
   d With the wind and the weather, and only the birds for company, it's a really _____ place.
   e I love watching the competitive spirit of the two teams. There's a really _____ atmosphere in the stadium.
   f The staff are really helpful, and it's easy to meet new people over a drink. It's a very _____ place.
   g What makes it easy to relax and think is how _____ it is. No noises or surprises.
   h I like the flowers: all bright yellows, reds and blues. It's a very _____ experience.

4 Replace each adjective in the sentences in exercise 3 with a near synonym from the list below.

> crowded ■ vibrant ■ boring ■ welcoming ■ quiet ■ sensuous ■ empty ■ remote

82

The individual and society

5 For each category a–c, think of a place where you go in your life to do these things.

a a place I go to have fun
b a place I go to relax
c a place I go to work or study
d a place I go to eat
e a place I go to be alone

6 With a partner, describe the places you chose using the adjectives in exercises 3 and 4. Explain your choice of adjectives.

Starting your description

1 🔊 2.35 Listen to three people describing a place which is important to them. Decide which speaker describes the types of places a–c. Make a note of any reasons they give for their choice.

Speaker 1: _____

Speaker 2: _____

Speaker 3: _____

a an urban place
b a domestic space
c a rural area

> **Technique**
>
> Practise using *where* and *which* in your description, e.g. 'A place which is exciting and where I go very often to have fun is …'. *Which* + adjective of description, *where* + activities you do.

2 🔊 2.35 Listen again and make a note of the expressions that each speaker uses to introduce the place they have chosen.

Speaker 1: _____

Speaker 2: _____

Speaker 3: _____

3 Read the Speaking Part 2 task card below. Take one minute to think and make notes about your own talk on this topic, using your own experience. Then practise speaking for two minutes using your notes.

> Describe a place which has influenced your life.
>
> You should say
>
> > where the place is
> >
> > what activities you normally do there
> >
> > what feelings you associate with the place
>
> and explain what influence the place has on your life.

> **Technique**
>
> Spend most time talking about the activities you do – this gives you more to say; the description of the place, using adjectives, will be quite short. In Part 2, you need to speak for 1–2 minutes.

83

Unit 10

Summing up impressions

1 In the last part of the Speaking Part 2 task card, you are normally asked to sum up your personal impressions. Match each mini-task 1–3 with the phrases a–g that you could use to answer it.

> 1 Describe a place where you spent a memorable holiday … and explain why it is particularly memorable.
>
> 2 Describe an experience in which you tried something new … and explain how you felt when you tried it.
>
> 3 Describe something special that you bought … and explain why this item is special to you.

a I remember it mainly because …/It was memorable because …
b It made me feel …
c The main reason for my reaction was …
d What I've learned from this is …
e The influence this has had on me is …
f This taught me an important lesson: …
g Its main effect on me has been …
h I feel attached to this … because …

2 Think of your answer to each of the mini-tasks in exercise 1. With a partner, give your answers, using the phrases above.

Pronunciation: using intonation in continuous speech

1 🔊 2.36 Listen to these three sentences. Decide if the intonation pattern of each sentence is a fall ↘ or a fall-rise ↘↗.

a I was a waiter.   c He was a dishwasher.
b I worked hard.   d The pay was poor.

2 🔊 2.37 Listen to this sentence and decide which part (A or B) has a fall or fall-rise intonation.

Part A: *I worked hard,*
Part B: *although the pay was poor.*

3 Link these sentence parts to make complete sentences, as spoken by a candidate in Part 1 of the Speaking Module.

	Part A		Part B
a	The pay was poor …	1	… but some were not.
b	I got the job …	2	… because I wanted to study more.
c	I worked long hours …	3	… although they were not very generous.
d	Some days were fun …	4	… because it was an unskilled job.
e	I got tips …	5	… but made good friends.
f	I gave it up …	6	… although I had no experience.

Technique

Use linking devices, and use their intonation to show how the parts of the sentences make a complete statement. This is continuous and connected speech. It will gain you marks for fluency.

4 🔊 2.38 Practise saying the sentences which you have made in exercise 3 using the fall-rise ↘↗ and fall ↘ intonation patterns. Listen and compare with the recording.

84

The individual and society

Exam listening

Section 3

🔊 2.39

Questions 21–24

Choose the correct letter, **A, B** *or* **C**.

21 Mike is concerned about their assignment because

    A there is too little time.
    B it's too difficult.
    C they have not prepared.

22 What aspect of social welfare does their assignment explore?

    A a survey of the whole subject
    B a definition of the main terms
    C a comparison of different approaches

23 Which approach to the assignment does Fiona recommend?

    A giving a personal view
    B taking a balanced approach
    C agreeing with the tutor

24 How long does the assignment have to be?

    A at least 2,000 words
    B at least 3,000 words
    C at least 4,000 words

🔊 2.40

Questions 25 and 26

Complete the sentences below.

Write **NO MORE THAN THREE WORDS** *for each answer.*

Professor Green's lecture is called **25** ....

It takes place in the Becket building at 10 a.m. on **26** ....

Questions 27–30

Complete the table below.

Write **NO MORE THAN TWO WORDS AND/OR A NUMBER** *for each answer.*

Title	Author	Publisher	Year
27	**28**	Glenfield University Press	2012
29 .... in Britain	Edward Jones	Polybus Publications	**30** ....

85

Phonemic Chart

iː w**ee**k	ɪ th**i**n	ʊ b**oo**k	uː sh**oo**t	ɪə h**ea**r	eɪ d**ay**	
e l**e**t	ə lat**er**	ɜː l**ear**n	ɔː f**or**	ʊə ma**tu**re	ɔɪ t**oy**	əʊ fl**ow**
æ m**a**p	ʌ f**u**n	ɑː f**ar**	ɒ st**o**p	eə f**ai**r	aɪ l**igh**t	aʊ d**ow**n
p **p**en	b **b**ite	t **t**own	d **d**o	tʃ **ch**eck	dʒ **j**am	k **c**an	g **g**o
f **f**ight	v **v**ery	θ **Th**ursday	ð **th**ey	s **s**ame	z **z**one	ʃ **sh**ut	ʒ lei**s**ure
m **m**ale	n **n**ight	ŋ ri**ng**	h **h**ot	l **l**ike	r **r**ight	w **w**ait	j **y**ear

Answer Key

UNIT 1

Topic talk

1
a Students' own answers.
b **Possible answer**
Students can be given grants by the government or they can be given vouchers to help subsidize their rent. They might also get financial help from their families.
c Students' own answers.

2
Students' own answers.

3
Students' own answers.

4
a penthouse
b house
c studio
d farmhouse
e bungalow
f terraced house
g shared house

5
1 a
2 d
3 c
4 g

6
a fascinating
b cramped
c modern
d bustling
e uncomfortable
f shabby
g boring

7
Students' own answers.

8
1 c
2 e
3 d
4 a
5 b

9
1 e
2 b
3 d
4 c
5 a

10
Reason because/with
Consequence so

11
Students' own answers.

Listening skills Predicting in tables

1
1 c
2 a
3 b

2
1 good
2 terraced houses
3 £125,000
4 18.2°C
5 612 mm
6 3567
7 £4.50
8 75%/25%
9 25%/75%

3
Tables 1 and 2 are read from left to right. Table 3 is read from top to bottom.

4
a Analogue and digital radios.
b Two.
c Five.
d 1, 4

5
a must be wrong: three words
b correct
c must be wrong: two numbers
d must be wrong: two words are acceptable, but two numbers are not

6
1 £95
2 stations
3 (sound) quality
4 1 year/one year
5 Battery life

Script
Customer I'm interested in buying a radio. Can you help me?
Assistant Yes, of course. As you can see, we have this analogue radio on special offer today for £29.99. They're normally £35. We've also got a much more modern range of digital radios – those are over there.
Customer Oh yes, digital radios, these are the modern ones.
Assistant Mmm, they're the new technology. This one, for example, sells at £95. The analogue radios are looking a bit old-fashioned now.
Customer But what is it that's better about the digital ones?
Assistant Well, the main advantage with the analogue ones is, of course, cheapness, but the main advantage with the digital ones is the number and variety of *stations* you can get – hundreds of them. All kinds of stations playing music – rock, pop, classical. Everything in fact, as well as news, current affairs, comedy … all sorts.
Customer What about the sound quality?
Assistant The quality is very good. Under certain circumstances, you can get amazing *sound quality* with analogue, but this is usually with very expensive radios which would normally be part of a hi-fi sound system – we have lots of those on the third floor if you're interested. The second great thing about digital is clarity: you get no interference, well, less interference than with analogue. You get a very clear and clean sound.
Customer Well, I want a radio for the flat I share with three other friends of mine.
Assistant In that case, you want something that will last. The analogues come with a *one-year* guarantee but the digitals have a two-year guarantee which is extendable to three years if you pay an extra £26. The main disadvantage with analogue is that it will be turned off in a few years – we don't know exactly when, but sometime.
Customer But what about the batteries? I've heard that they use a lot of batteries.
Assistant That is probably the one disadvantage of the digital radios. The *battery life* is not very long, but they all come with rechargeable batteries, which really solves the problem.

87

7

a The numbers suggest that the speakers will discuss each category (on the left) in turn. That is, they will compare both the old ValueCard and the new SuperValue Card with regard to Points. Then they will compare them with regard to credit period, and so on.

b All missing information appears to be numerical. You cannot predict any of the answers exactly, but you may be able to predict that the numbers will be within a certain range.

8

6 3/three
7 22.5
8 1/one
9 20/twenty
10 12

Script

Assistant So, how would you like to pay?
Customer Er, cash?
Assistant Do you have a Robson's Store Card?
Customer I think I might do. Here we are.
Assistant Oh my goodness, I haven't seen one of those for a long time. Those are the old ValueCards. Now you can get a SuperValue Card, which is even better value.
Customer Really? I don't know what to do.
Assistant Well, I can change you onto a SuperValue Card if you want. With the SuperValue Card you get double the standard number of points, and your free credit period is longer. With your old card you get one month's free credit, but you can get *three* months' free credit with the new card. The interest rate is a bit higher, at *22.5 per cent* rather than 18.5 per cent, but if you're careful you don't have to pay interest at all.
Customer Well, I'm not sure about that – it seems better in some ways. Can I continue to use my old card?
Assistant You certainly can, until they withdraw them, which I'm sure they will before too long. But with the SuperValue Card there are special cardholder-only days – two per month, compared with *one* per month with the old card.
Customer I see. My old card gave me free delivery, too.
Assistant That's right, free delivery within *twenty* miles. The SuperValue Card gives you free delivery up to 50 miles.
Customer That sounds good. I think the old card was free, too.

Assistant Mmm, with the SuperValue card there is an initial fee of just £12, and then it's very good value.
Customer I think I'll pay cash.
Assistant Very good, madam.

Speaking skills Identifying yourself

1

Script

a Can you tell me your full name?
b And what shall I call you?
c Where do you come from?
d Could you show me your ID?

2

Candidate Hello, good *afternoon*.
Examiner Good *afternoon*. Can you *tell* me your *full* name, please?
Candidate My name is *Benjamin Weiss*.
Examiner And what can I *call* you?
Candidate Please *call* me *Ben*.
Examiner Good. Where *do* you come *from*?
Candidate I come *from Switzerland*.
Examiner Can you *show* me your identification, please?
Candidate Of course. *Here* is my *passport*.

3

Students' own answers.

Discussing familiar topics

1

1 f
2 c
3 g
4 d
5 b
6 h
7 a
8 e

2

a They relate to personal information.
b Answers a, d, f, g and h are especially good.
In a and f, there is a short answer followed by a further (short) description.
In g and h, there is a direct answer followed by an explanation.
In d, a direct answer is followed by further relevant information.

3

b Where was the last place you travelled to?
c What form of transport do you use most?
d When did you start learning English?
e Which form of communication do you like to use most – email or phone?
f What sports have you played?
g What kind of food do you like to eat?
h What hobbies do you have?

i What sort of television programmes do you enjoy watching?
j What type of books do you enjoy reading?

4

Students' own answers.

Saying where you come from

1

1 Could you tell me something about where you live?
2 What sort of place is that?
3 Is there anything you particularly like about it?
4 And what kind of jobs do people do there?

Script

Examiner Now, in this first part I'd like to ask you some questions about yourself. Let's talk about your town or village.
Candidate OK.
Examiner Could you tell me *something about where you live*?
Candidate Yes. I used to live in Switzerland but I've recently moved to the UK. Now I live in Weybridge.
Examiner What *sort of place is that*?
Candidate It's a large, busy place. It's near London. It has got lots and lots of people and houses – it's typical of a London suburb.
Examiner Is there anything *you particularly like about it*?
Candidate The great thing about Weybridge is the facilities. You've got everything you need: shops, buses and trains, cinemas, pubs and restaurants, entertainment. You never need to leave it! You've got all you want!
Examiner I see. And what kind *of jobs do people do there*?
Candidate All kinds. I suppose mostly people work in offices, for big companies. Some people work in shops. There are a lot of high tech companies around there.
Examiner Thank you. Now let's talk about what you do …

2

1 moved here from Switzerland recently
2 large, busy place, near London – lots of people and houses – typical London suburb
3 the facilities – he gives a list of them
4 they work in offices, companies, shops, high tech companies

In questions 1 and 2, the candidate gives extra information.

Answer Key

In answer to questions 3 and 4, the candidate gives a short answer and then gives examples.

3
Students' own answers.

4
Students' own answers.

Pronunciation: stressing syllables

1
pleasant 2
dynamic 3
flat 1
peaceful 2
cramped 1
bungalow 3
detached 2
overpriced 3

2
Pattern 1 flat, cramped
Pattern 2 pleasant, peaceful
Pattern 3 detached
Pattern 4 bungalow
Pattern 5 dynamic
Pattern 6 overpriced

3
a also; stress on 1st syllable, not on 2nd
b interest; stress on 1st syllable, not on 2nd
c solution; stress on 2nd syllable, not on 1st
d afternoon; stress on 3rd syllable, not on 2nd
e information; stress on 3rd syllable, not on 2nd
f analysis; stress on 2nd syllable, not on 3rd
g communicable; stress on 2nd syllable, not on 3rd.

Exam listening

Questions 11–15
11 – 13 IN ANY ORDER:
full-time students
part-time students
distance learners: … *there may be a few distance learners on the tour today*.
14 make an appointment: … *if you want to visit it (i.e. the Fieldhouse Library) you will need to make an appointment.*
15 (your) ID card: … *to gain access to the facilities you must have your ID card.*

Script

Librarian Good morning. My name is Mandy and I am going to tell you a little about the John R Jones Memorial Library here at Blackwater College. We regard the library as a gateway to the resources that you as students at the College may need. The majority of you are *full-time students* – you may find you spend a lot of time here. Even those of you who are *part-time students* will no doubt require the services too. I hope that by the end of this short talk you will know the services the library has to offer, including the website, and how to get any further help you may need. Sorry, I forgot there may be a few *distance learners* on the tour today. I'll explain about the online facilities and borrowing by post scheme a little later on. This is the main site of the library, but we also have the Rivergate building and the Fieldhouse Library. The Rivergate building houses the geography resources, that is the book collection and the journal collection, as well as the map collection. The hours and days of opening of the Rivergate collection are the same as this building except that it's closed on Christmas Day and New Year's Day. The Fieldhouse Library contains a specialist collection of local history and if you want to visit it you will need to *make an appointment*. Those two facilities are the only exceptions to the rule that all the Blackwater College libraries are open 24 hours a day, seven days a week, 365 days a year. However, *to gain access to the facilities you must have your ID card* – no ID card, no entry. We have heard all the stories and excuses and we don't accept any of them. Just remember your ID card!

Questions 16–20
16 Economics: …*we are currently moving the Economics collection here …*
17 French Literature: … *we will be moving the French Literature collection into this building next week*
18 new restaurant: … *we are still building the new restaurant* (Maximum of 2 words allowed in this answer)
19 150: *We have recently updated 150 computer stations …*
20 national newspapers: … *there is a wide range of national newspapers available from the librarians on request.*

Script

Librarian Now, I must apologize for the mess you can see around you today. Libraries should be quiet places, but unfortunately this is not currently the case here. This new building has been here for only two months, and as a result we have not quite finished moving in! So far, we have moved most of the book and journal collections from the old library into this new building. There are two exceptions: we are currently moving the *Economics* collection here, which should be installed by tomorrow, and we will be moving the *French Literature* collection into this building next week. But, as you can see, we are still building the *new restaurant*. We will finish it, we hope, very shortly. We have finished the café, however, and students can use it during the library opening hours. We have recently updated *150* computer stations and we will be adding another one hundred shortly, so that there will be plenty for everybody soon. Very shortly this library will be one of the finest in this part of the country. Don't forget that the library isn't just about academic books. In addition to the books and journals there is a wide range of *national newspapers* available from the librarians on request. I'd like to mention the different ways you can get help in using our resources. Don't forget our website at www.mlbc.ac.uk. There you can access the full catalogues, and also journals if you have your password and ID number. Now, any questions?

UNIT 2

Topic talk

1

Possible answers
a The plane ticket probably reminds the speaker of a memorable journey. The musician perhaps triggers memories of a special event. The photo on the phone probably reminds the speaker of a special pet.
b The memories are happy, because of the adjective *unforgettable*.
c Students' own answers.
d Students' own answers.

2
a marvellous great
b happy remarkable
c great momentous
d memorable favourable
e exhilarating rewarding
f exciting big
g outstanding impressive
h golden happy
i fantastic great

3

Possible answers
thoroughly: exciting, memorable, impressive

89

highly: rewarding, exciting
very: happy, exhilarating, rewarding, big, impressive, favourable
totally: happy, exhilarating, rewarding, outstanding

4
a an experience
b an achievement
c an event
d a special occasion
e an adventure

5
Possible answers
an achievement: I came first in the school swimming gala.
an event: I went to an open-air music concert.
an occasion: I attended my sister's twenty-first birthday party.
an experience: I worked for several months in a bank.
an adventure: I travelled around Europe on my own.

6
Students' own answers.

7
a rewarding experience
b unforgettable moment
c bizarre incident
d memorable trip
e formal occasion
f nerve-racking adventure
g exhilarating experience
h humbling experience

8
Students' own answers.

Listening skills Understanding signpost phrases

1
Starting: e, h
Listing: c, f, h
Adding: a, i
Digressing: d
Returning to the subject: b
Concluding: c, g

2
b; e; d; a; g; c; f

Answering sentence completion questions

1
a false   d false
b true   e true
c true   f true

2
See answers to 1.

3
1 2/two: It deals with two general topics.
2 economics: … *and we have some students of economics with us also* …
3 exciting: … *I find it exciting.*

Script
Lecturer Good morning, everybody. I'd like to begin this term's lectures with a discussion of the various sub-disciplines in history. Before I do that though, can I refer you to the handout you picked up on the way in? It deals with *two* general topics. The first is 'Why study history?' and the second is 'What is history?'. Neither of these questions has an easy answer. In fact, people have been asking these questions for as long as history has been studied. However, as you are mostly new students to this subject – and we have some students of *economics* with us also – I feel you should have some background to these basic questions. Anyway, it's all in the handout. I might add that for me personally, the most important reason for studying history is that I find it *exciting*. Our ancestors can remain, if we want them to, a mystery, a closed book, a blackness that we never see into. Or, we can come to know what motivated them and discover how that led to the world we live in today.

Answering matching questions

1
1 B   4 C
2 B   5 B
3 A   6 B

2
You can predict that *post-modern history* does not sound *traditional*; *political history* and *military history* sound traditional; and *feminist history* sounds modern.

3

Words in the question	Possible words in the recording
traditional	old-fashioned, orthodox, classical, conventional
modern	present-day, contemporary, new, up-to-date, current
looks to the future	progressive, forward-looking

4
4 T: *Traditionally, history was seen as one subject … This is what we now call political history.*

5 F: … *progressive areas of study are as much about what should happen in the future. One example of this is the field of post-modern history.*
6 F: *Likewise, feminist history looks at the past to make sure the future will be different …*
7 M: … *a range of areas of study which have developed over the modern period … You can study social history …*
8 M: … *or economic history.*
9 T: *one area of conventional history which … has had a resurgence of interest in recent years is the area of military history.*
10 M: … *examples of kinds of history which … differ from the orthodox forms. … Ethnic history is a present-day concern …*

Script
Lecturer You who have chosen to pursue the study of history are very fortunate. This is a time when we can talk not just about history but histories. Traditionally, history was seen as one subject and the subject matter was clear. It was about kings and queens and wars. Additionally, it was about states and empires or groups of states. This is what we now call political history. The sub-topics were the parts of the world – for example, the history of China or of France. History has moved on somewhat, and we can learn a lot about current views of history by looking at the proposed lecture topics in our leading universities. In fact, you'll see that even the simplest definition of history – that it is about what happened in the past – is up for grabs. Some of the more, how shall I put it, progressive areas of study are as much about what should happen in the future. One example of this is the field of post-modern history. Likewise, feminist history looks at the past to make sure the future will be different, and it uses the past to assist in its efforts to make the future as it wants it to be. Somewhere in the middle of these two extremes lie a range of areas of study which have developed over the modern period, replacing the traditional idea of political history. These are by now mostly well established. You can study social history or economic history. Social history asks about ordinary people and their lives. Not just their daily lives but their contribution to changes in our society. Ordinary people have desires

Answer Key

and wishes which they try to put into effect and this has a massive impact on social development, which was not fully understood in the classical study of history. By the way, one area of conventional history which I forgot to mention, but which has had a resurgence of interest in recent years, is the area of military history. This was, of course, of great practical use in more violent times and unfortunately has become of increasing use and interest – academically and practically – in our own times. By the way, there is a new series of lectures on military history in our department – as if to demonstrate the truth of what I have just said. Ethnic and multi-cultural history are further examples of kinds of history which, like social history, differ from the orthodox forms. Ethnic history is a present-day concern which concentrates on the value systems and beliefs of a people – usually a minority people – which were ignored in the rapid forward march of the rich and powerful nations and states. How various ethnic groups live together and how their traditions change and develop is the subject of its contemporary cousin, multi-cultural history. In summary, as I said, you are fortunate to have such a wide choice of things to study in the fields of history. Choose wisely. And finally, it only remains for me to wish you good luck in your studies.

Speaking skills Describing a past event

1
Possible answers
a Found – in a shop window
   Lost – in a newspaper, shop window
b The purse owner may find the purse, with or without the cards, especially if she has lost it near the shop, and sees the notice. The wallet owner may be less lucky. The finder may not want the trouble of phoning.
c 30 per cent as a reward seems reasonable. However, £10 is not a lot of money, so maybe a finder will keep the wallet, rather than claim the reward.
d Students' own answers.

2
Students' own answers.

3
He lost his car. It was very important to him – the most precious, beautiful, wonderful thing.

Script
I should say, and, yes, this is something I forgot to say, this car was *the most precious, beautiful, wonderful thing* in my life at that time. And there I was. Without it. I'd lost it. I felt very … how shall I put it? … stupid. Now, where was I? Oh yes, talking to the policeman. He didn't really take any notice of me. He didn't laugh, but he did look very uninterested. Now next, … let me see … yes, the next thing that happened was that …

Informal speech: using signpost phrases

1
a 3   c 1
b 4   d 2

Planning your talk in Part 2

1
a Losing an important thing.
b Five in total: 1 instruction in the opening sentence. Then, 4 detailed mini-instructions after that.
c One instruction relates to the present; the others relate to the past.

2
Possible answers
1 What efforts you made to find it, i.e. you went to a shop.
2 What efforts you made to find it, i.e. you also went to the police.
3 What you will do in the future, i.e. buy a bag with a shoulder strap which is less easy to lose.
4 Describing the important thing, i.e. the handbag.
5 Why the thing was important to you, i.e. it contained cash and/or credit cards.
6 What efforts you made to find it, i.e. you put an advertisement in a newspaper.
7 How you lost it, i.e. you think you lost it in a shop.

3
Possible answer
I remember one time when I lost a handbag. *Well, I should say first that* it was probably my own fault. *Looking back, I realize that* I had a habit of putting it down. I think I lost it in a shop. It had all my cards in it, so I was desperate. Anyway, *to find it, I first* went back to the shop, but they couldn't help. *After that, I* went to the police. They suggested I put an ad in the newspaper, so *finally*, that's what *I* did. *In future, I won't* use a handbag. I'll always use a bag with a shoulder strap.

4
Students' own answers.

Describing precautions

1
in case

2
a 1 In future, I will keep some keys in a flowerpot in the front garden in case I lose my house keys.
b 3 In future, I will keep a paper map in the car in case my GPS gives me wrong information.
c 2 In future, I will note the phone number of my embassy in case I lose my passport.
d 6 In future, I will put a second umbrella in the car in case I leave mine at home.
e 5 In future, I will bring a packet of sweets in case my ears start to pop in the plane.
f 4 In future, I will write down the phone number of my bank in case I lose my credit card.

3
Students' own answers.

Pronunciation: linking in connected speech

1a
car~engine
rare~opportunity
amateur~actor
summer~activity
for~ever
fire~escape
fire~alarm
b Students' own answers.

2 a
bigger~and better
more~and more
quicker~and quicker
wider~and longer
b Students' own answers.

3a
nearly /j/ always
key /j/ ingredient
new /w/ idea
every /j/ opportunity
too /w/ easy
very /j/ often
b Students' own answers.

4a
not /tʃ/ yet
told /dʒ/ you so
not /tʃ/ usually
not /tʃ/ yours
mind /dʒ/ you
heard /dʒ/ you the first time
b Students' own answers.

91

5
This happened about a year /r/ ago. I had chosen a pullover /r/ in a shop. I joined the queue /w/ at the cash desk. 'Could /dʒ/ you put the card in the machine, please?' the shop assistant said. I looked for my card but I couldn't find it. 'I know I had it /tʃ/ yesterday,' I thought. My face became redder /r/ and redder. I said, 'I'm sorry /j/ about this. I'll leave the pullover here.' I rushed out of the store, very /j/ embarrassed.

6 Students' own answers.

Exam listening

Questions 21–25
21 costs, benefits
22 size
23 raise money
24 100
25 (display) cabinets

Script

Anne Hello Tom!
Tom Hello Anne!
Anne What have you been doing?
Tom Oh, just sitting around, catching up with some reading.
Anne I've had a great time. You know we're doing this assignment on … what is it?
Tom 'Museums – their *costs* and *benefits*.'
Anne That's right. Well, I've been to the Sandgate Museum. It was really good. These local museums are really interesting because they connect people with the history of one special place. We all know about kings and emperors and battles and wars, but local museums tell us about the everyday lives of ordinary people and that's why they are so important.
Tom I'm not so sure about that. I think they are of interest but they're so small that they can't give a true picture of things. They do their best.
Anne I don't really agree. They do give a true picture, but perhaps not a full picture. It's the truth but not the whole truth.
Tom I think the *size* is the number one problem. Because they're small and local they attract few visitors. That's why they have so little money. And because they have little money they can't buy or maintain many really interesting exhibits. As a result, the shop is almost as big as the museum to try to *raise money* by selling souvenirs, postcards, sweets, and so on.
Anne I think they find it difficult, but not impossible. And don't forget, they get a lot of their exhibits free from local people. There was this boat, for example, that was fantastic!
Tom Really? What was that?
Anne There was a massive fishing boat, a real one, *about a hundred years* old, and you could walk on it, and get the feeling of what fishing in those days was really like.
Tom Mmm, sounds quite good. But I've always found that these kinds of museums are a bit dingy. For example, the *display cabinets* are so dark that you can hardly see the exhibits, and the labels are sometimes difficult to read …

Questions 26–30
26 B Tom: … *that should come from the local authority* …
27 C Tom: …*Why? … They could survive from donations* …
28 A Tom: … *The state should spend more on science museums* …
29 C Anne: … *a sort of museum which should not get public funds is the craft museum.*
Tom: … *Yes* …
30 B Tom: … *But a working farm is a different thing again …. That's the sort of thing that the local government should be spending its money on.*

Script

Anne So coming back to our assignment. What we've got to decide is whether these museums should be funded by the government or just by local people.
Tom I think it depends entirely on what kind of museum it is.
Anne How do you mean?
Tom Well, take local history museums. They're small so they won't survive without financial support. But *that should come from the local authority*, since only people in that area or tourists will visit it.
Anne I agree, but what about big natural history museums? Surely they should get money from the central government.
Tom Why? Children who want to learn about nature can go out into the countryside with their schoolteachers. *They could survive from donations*, and they get loads of visitors anyway. *The state should spend more on science museums*, since not enough people are studying science these days.
Anne I'm not so sure. But I do think *a sort of museum which should not get public funds is the craft museum*.
Tom Yes, like museums of cotton weaving.
Anne Yeah, which are of interest to only a very small number of people, and they should pay for it.
Tom I agree. *But a working farm is a different thing again*. That's something from all of our pasts and so it's important to the local community. Kids can learn a lot too. *That's the sort of thing that the local government should be spending its money on*.
Anne Yes, I agree. Well, I think we've got plenty of ideas for our assignment.

Unit 3

Topic talk

1

Possible answers
The camera could be damaged or broken; the jumper could be ripped or torn; the pages of the book could be torn and the cover damaged.

2

Possible answers
a Some people think it isn't, because their card number might not be secure.
b The main effects are that most goods are cheaper. However, such shopping means that certain smaller businesses are closing.
c Students' own answers.
d Students' own answers.

3
a, c and d match camera; a camera doesn't have a lid

4
cloth: cotton, linen, silk
metal: gold, aluminium, brass, tin, steel
man-made: polyester, glass, plastic

5

Possible answers
spherical: globe
rectangular: laptop
square: table
circular: DVD
oval: plate
spiral: staircase

6
Students' own answers.

7
1 g   5 a
2 b   6 d
3 e   7 h
4 f   8 c

Answer Key

8
a ripped
b leaking
c jammed
d faded
e cracked
f snapped
g scratched
h uncomfortable
i twisted
j wobbly

9
Possible answers
a You sent me these trousers, and I was really annoyed to find that the trouser leg was completely ripped.
b When I opened the food blender you sent, I found the bowl was leaking very badly.

Listening skills Understanding information in flow charts

1
1 c 3 d
2 a 4 b

2

As a result	cause and effect
This means that	cause and effect
If …, then	conditional
Firstly	linear ordering
Otherwise	conditional
Next	linear ordering
Unless … , then	conditional
This leads to	cause and effect
Finally,	linear ordering
If not, then	conditional
To begin with	linear ordering

3
You would expect to hear phrases for linear ordering and conditionals. Phrases for linear ordering could occur at any stage, although *firstly* and *finally* are more restricted to the beginning and end. Phrases for conditionals would occur at question points where two alternatives are available. Phrases for cause and effect are less likely in this flow chart, but may be common in flow charts that detail natural processes.

4
a Starting point: customer complains about malfunction
End point: customer has working product and is satisfied
b product repairs, product malfunction, customer complaints
c customer (5 times); product (4 times)
d *firstly, finally, to begin with,* and *next*, since a flow chart describes a sequence of actions; *otherwise, if …, then, if not, then,* where there is a question with *yes* or *no* as possible answers.

5
1 repair centre: *It goes off to a repair centre.*
2 (an) estimate: *… we will get back an estimate of how much it will cost and how long it will take.*
3 agree: *It's your decision entirely whether you agree.*
4 collect: *… arrange a time for you to collect it from us.*
5 3/three: *… return it to your home address within three days.*

Script
Assistant Good morning, madam. Can I help you?
Customer Yes, please. I bought this breadmaking machine from you quite a while ago and it doesn't work.
Assistant I see. That's unusual. These breadmakers are usually very reliable. You didn't overfill it, did you? Or put too much water in the mix? Those are two reasons for malfunction we often hear of.
Customer No. Certainly not. I had it working for quite a while and then it stopped working. It doesn't do anything now.
Assistant I see. That sounds like a fault in the machine.
Customer Yes. I wonder if you can do anything about it for me.
Assistant Well, that depends. If it is inside the guarantee period we can help you. Otherwise, it will be more difficult.
Customer Let me see. I have the receipt here. I bought it in – it was some time ago – the receipt says, … in February last year.
Assistant February. Well, unfortunately that means it is outside the warranty period. In that case, I'll get you a form which you can fill in and we'll see what we can do.
Customer Well, what can you do, do you think?
Assistant Well, as I say, if you fill in this form, we can send away the breadmaker to be mended. It goes off to a *repair centre*.
Customer Oh good. What happens then?
Assistant Then, we don't get an exact costing, but we will get back an *estimate* of how much it will cost and how long it will take.
Customer I see. And do you think it will be expensive?
Assistant Well, it won't be cheap. There will be labour and parts to think about and also the postage and packing costs.
Customer And we don't know how much they will be?
Assistant Not yet. But when you get the estimate, you've got two options, obviously. If you agree, you can go ahead. Or if you don't, you can say, 'No, it's too expensive'. It's your decision entirely whether you *agree*.
Customer And if I go ahead?
Assistant Then we arrange the repair. We don't have much stock room, so when it is done what we'll have to do is arrange a time for you *to collect* it from us.
Customer All right, that's what I'll do.
Assistant Just give me the receipt.
Customer Here you are.
Assistant Just a minute, madam. I thought you said you bought the breadmaker in February.
Customer That's right. Here is the date. Two – twelve – thirteen
Assistant I think there's some mistake. In the UK, two twelve thirteen is the second of December two thousand and thirteen.
Customer Oh, of course. How stupid of me! Of course it is!
Assistant So it's inside the warranty period.
Customer Oh great.
Assistant That's right. That's much easier.
Customer So, what can you do now?
Assistant Very simple. You fill in this form, we replace the machine and return it to your home address within *three* days.
Customer Well, that's excellent.

6
6 217980345
7 Yonge
8 15
9 Capercaillie
10 Monday

Script
Assistant Now, let me have your details.
Customer Certainly.
Assistant Now – this is a Gleeware … Breadmaker 3 … model number?
Customer I have it here – two – one – seven …
Assistant *Two – one – seven …*
Customer *nine – eight – zero …*
Assistant nine – eight – oh
Customer *three – four – five.*
Assistant Thank you. Now, where did you buy it – was it here?
Customer No, it was in your shop in Bluewater.
Assistant I see … Bluewater – date bought – two – twelve – thirteen. Now can I have your name?
Customer Yes. It's *Yonge*, J H Yonge.

93

Assistant That's …
Customer That's spelled Y-O-N-GE, that's Yonge.
Assistant I see. And your address?
Customer *15 Capercaillie* Gardens, Aberdeen.
Assistant Er, I should know this, can you tell me …
Customer Yes, it's C-A-P-E-R then C-A-I-double-L-I-E.
Assistant Sorry, could you say that again?
Customer Sure. C-A-P-E-R-CA-I-double-L-I-E.
Assistant And Gardens as in Gardens.
Customer Yes.
Assistant Good. And the postcode?
Customer AD22 4SC.
Assistant Thank you. And what would be a convenient time of day to deliver the replacement breadmaker?
Customer Morning is best, if that's all right?
Assistant That's fine. So it should be with you on *Monday*, madam.
Customer Good. Thank you very much. Bye.
Assistant Goodbye, madam.

Speaking skills Answering part 3 discussion questions

1
Students' own answers.

2
Students' own answers.

3
Students' own answers.

4
2d 3e 4b 5c 6a 7h 8g

5
Speaker 1: 8, Which do you prefer, shopping in local markets or shopping in big stores?
Speaker 2: 7, In what ways does discarded packaging cause serious environmental problems?
Speaker 3: 2, To what extent is shopping a form of relaxation?

Script
Speaker 1 <u>I suppose that</u> the main difference is that it's set up to be a lot more convenient. It's easy to go and park up at a supermarket and get all your shopping in one go. I know a lot of people don't approve of that. Nevertheless, <u>from my point of view</u>, it's a really good thing. I can save time.

Speaker 2 <u>To my mind</u>, we worry far too much these days about what things are wrapped in. It's all about marketing really. Some customers expect to buy their toothpaste tube in a box, but what's the point? <u>It seems to me that</u> we need to change attitudes about this.

Speaker 3 Well, <u>from my point of view</u>, it's completely the opposite. It just gets me stressed. But I know for a lot of people it's a form of leisure activity. They'd rather wander round a shopping centre than go to a park or the beach. <u>Personally, I think</u> it's a really odd attitude.

6
Students' own answers.

Introducing opinions

1
Speaker 1: I suppose that; from my point of view
Speaker 2: To my mind; it seems to me that
Speaker 3: from my point of view; Personally, I think

2
Students' own answers.

3
Students' own answers.

4
a Keeping up with the Joneses
b The fashion cycle
c You are what you wear

5
Students' own answers.

Pronunciation: using opinion phrases

1
a In <u>my</u> view,
b To <u>my</u> mind,
c It seems to <u>me</u> that
d <u>My</u> impression is that

2
The pronouns *my* and *me* carry the main stress.

3
Students' own answers.

Exam listening

Questions 31–35
31 designers: *… the major responsibility must be borne by designers.*
32 materials: *… but rather that of Materials Acquisition.*
33 fishing: *… harvesting, which includes the cutting down of trees as a first step in the making of furniture or paper, or fishing.*
34 waste: *… as with all chemical processes, waste is produced …*
35 manufacturing: *… a lot of manufacturing seems unnecessary if we could only organize things better.*

Script
Lecturer I'm going to begin my lecture today with a look at Product Life Cycles. Now, as we go through the Product Life Cycle I'll be trying to raise some issues which are important with regard to each phase of the cycle. I won't have all the answers for you this morning. This one of the lecture series is just to get you started and – I hope – interested. Let's start with the first phase of the cycle, that of Product Design. This is really the most important part of the cycle. We often talk as if it is consumers who are responsible for recycling – and so they are – but in reality the major responsibility must be borne by *designers*. They can design products where recycling is easy and cheap, or difficult and expensive. In the latter case, the likelihood is that recycling – though technically feasible – will not, in fact, take place. Now don't jump ahead, because the second stage is not Product Manufacturing, but rather that of *Materials* Acquisition. This is the activity we do when we mine coal or other minerals such as gold or iron or copper. In addition to mining, there is harvesting, which includes the cutting down of trees as a first step in the making of furniture or paper, or *fishing*. These activities have costs which are not only monetary: pollution is one of the extra costs. We have also to think whether the resources we use are renewable – such as trees – or not – such as coal and other minerals. The third stage is not manufacturing either. It is Materials Processing. This is where we take the raw materials and use energy to change them into a form that can be used in manufacturing. For example, trees must be turned into paper, or oil into plastic. The cotton plants that grow in the fields must be turned into cloth. All of these activities require the use of chemical processes and, as with all chemical processes, *waste* is produced – often of a dangerous kind. And now we come to the Manufacturing stage. This is usually the most expensive in terms of cost and energy and waste. The wastes are often those that contribute to global climate change. For example,

Answer Key

we make 41 billion glass containers (mostly bottles) each year and we throw most of them away: a lot of *manufacturing* seems unnecessary if we could only organize things better. And this could mean greater profits for the manufacturing companies, too. Stage five is Packaging. Many products are packed in paper or plastic which themselves, of course, have their own processes and costs. Excessive packaging is often criticized, but it must be remembered that packaging serves a purpose – often more than one purpose – such as maintaining freshness and hygiene, as well as providing *information*. In our globalized world, we must never forget the next stage, which is Distribution. This is the stage where transportation and energy play a big part. Lorries, trucks, trains, planes and ships all use up the precious stocks of oil and, as we know, generate greenhouse gases which, as we hear again and again, contribute to climate change. Stage seven is the point of it all: using the product. Looking after products, using them in the recommended ways, timely repair and maintenance, all reduce the need for early replacement and reduce the number of products in landfill sites. We should not encourage the purchase of *single use* products, that is, products which are designed for use on one occasion only, and then to be thrown away and replaced. I'm going to skip a stage for a moment and move straight on to the final stage which is Disposal – putting the product in the bin. This is the end of the life of the product and we lose it completely. It may have only a little value but it does have a *value* even at this stage of its life, even in fact when it's actually in the landfill site. Now, I missed out one stage. This is a cycle within a cycle. That is, within the life cycle of the product there can be a closed loop cycle which can extract more value from the product. This is the reuse and recycle loop. It is a closed loop because, in theory, it can continue forever, though in practice of course, this is not possible. Recycling products means that they can be used to make more of the same product – CDs, bottles, books – or that they can be used to make different ones. For example, one pound of recycled paper can make six *cereal boxes*. And if we recycled all our newspapers, there could be a *saving of 40,000 trees* a day! Now, with this approach to the life cycle of a product in mind, we can go on to consider Life Cycle Analysis …

Questions 36–40
36 information: *… as well as providing information.*
37 single use: *We should not encourage the purchase of single use products …*
38 value: *… it does have a value even at this stage of its life, even in fact when it's actually in the landfill site.*
39 cereal boxes: *… one pound of recycled paper can make six cereal boxes.*
40 saving *… there could be a saving of 40,000 trees a day.*

UNIT 4
Topic talk
1
a It is a seminar. In a tutorial, a lecturer/tutor gives academic advice to a student or a couple of students. In a seminar, a group of students and a lecturer talk about a subject from a lecture or students present a paper on a chosen subject to their peers. In a lecture, students listen to a lecturer talk about a particular subject.
b Students' own answers.
c Students' own answers.

2
a requirements
b criteria
c programme
d module
e paper
f portfolio
g analysis
h evaluation
i essay
j dissertation

3
a fulfil
b meet
c enrol (on)
d choose
e submit
f present
g carry out
h make
i submit
j submit

4
a academic paper, in-depth analysis, critical evaluation, long essay
b assessment criteria, core module, portfolio of their work, MA dissertation

5
Possible answers
d set out your hypothesis and explain your terms of reference
g state your aims and objectives
f provide a survey of existing literature
c describe the methods used for collecting data
a present an analysis of the data
e draw conclusions based on your analysis
b include a bibliography

6
a background reading list
b research project
c easy-going tutors
d end-of-year examination
e deadlines; extensions
f individual tuition
g ongoing assessment
h practical work
i vocational content
j weekly seminars

7
Students' own answers.

8
Students' own answers.

Listening skills Identifying campus contexts
1
Possible answers
a books, CDs, DVDs, researchers, librarians, photocopier, computers
b kitchen, lounge, bicycles, Internet connection
c seats, whiteboard, steps, platform, lights, sound system
d apparatus, test tube, bench, sink, stool, notes, lab coat

2
Possible answers
1 The most likely place for students to have a discussion is a *student flat*, followed by *lecture theatre* and *library*.
2 The least likely answer is *drinking coffee*, since this is unlikely to take all morning. *Studying* is the most likely answer, followed by *training*.

Using information in multiple-choice questions
1
a At least two, since Bill and Chloe are mentioned by name.
b Bill – question 4 mentions his assignment.
c Psychology or education.
d Stages in child development.

95

2
1 B   3 C
2 C   4 B

Script
Bill It was packed! There simply aren't enough seats in Theatre 4 – there were people on the stairs, people in the aisles – I don't imagine everybody was able to get in.

Chloe Was Jack with you?

Bill No, of course not. I saw him with a pile of journals in the library as I walked past. You haven't seen him because you've been here in the kitchen drinking coffee all morning whereas he's been studying hard.

Chloe Not me! I've been in my bedroom reading for my assignment on education in the classical world – very interesting. It was easier than I expected. I should have been at the gym training for my next race, but that'll have to wait. And did you find your first lecture interesting?

Bill Absolutely fascinating! We talked about this experiment: if you show a child a litre of water in a bucket and show him a litre of water in a tall container, he always thinks the higher, taller but narrower container has more water in it.

Chloe Hold on, what do you show him?

Bill Right. You show him two things: a bucket … with a litre of water in it. And also, a tall, glass, vase-like thing or any tall container – this also has a litre of water in it. Now, he will say that the tall thing has more in it than the short fat thing, that is, the bucket. And all children will say this, that is, up to about five years of age. You can then actually pour a litre of water from the bucket into the taller, narrower container and the child will still say that the tall container contains more water – even though he has just seen the water come out of the bucket!

Chloe And what's the point of that? Is it about measurement?

Bill No, it showed how children are quite unable to think logically. It's connected with my assignment. It's about cognitive development of young children over time. That's to say it's about how they think. But didn't you do that assignment last year?

Chloe No, I didn't. You see, I missed out on the first year when I changed subject.

Answering summary completion questions

1
Students' own answers.

2
Students' own answers.

3
a Chloe.
b Her likes and dislikes.

4
a 8   d 5
b 6   e 7
c 10   f 9

5
5 second
6 criminal
7 rules; exceptions
8 international trade
9 famous cases
10 practical

Script
Chloe I started psychology in the *second* year – which is where I am now.

Bill Lucky you.

Chloe I'm not so sure. I've missed out on a lot of the basic stuff like that, and I will have to catch up in my own time. So I'm relying on you!

Bill Oh yes, I remember. What did you study before you changed?

Chloe I studied law.

Bill Why didn't you continue?

Chloe I found some of the subjects interesting enough – in fact, the *criminal* area was fascinating in general. But a lot of the law is very technical. It's full of little details, which can be very difficult to understand. And I've got a terrible memory too. I could never get all the *rules* and *exceptions* into my head. My number one hate really was *international trade* which was a minefield of rules and exceptions – in fact I think it was a complete nightmare!

Bill But law is such a popular subject – lots of people would like to study it.

Chloe I'm sure they would, but they often don't realize that it's very book-based. You spend most of your time reading about *famous cases* sitting in a stuffy library and very occasionally you get out – to a lecture, or maybe a seminar!

Bill What do you find that's better about psychology?

Chloe Most of all I like the experimental psychology we have to study. This involves doing something, so it's *practical*, and with any luck you can make a small – OK very small – contribution to knowledge. And it's so useful in many careers, for example, business, commerce, education …

Bill Law is too, you know.

Chloe Yes, but the training is so long. You have to spend at least another two years on a professional practice course before you can start working. No, I'm happy with psychology.

Bill Well, as a psychology student, too, I must say I agree with absolutely everything you've said, of course …

Speaking skills Describing people

1
Students' own answers.

2
1c   6h
2j   7d
3g   8f
4a   9e
5i   10b

3a
Possible answers

Audible	U
Demanding	I
Conscientious	I
Positive	I
Polite	N
Knowledgeable	I
Strict	U
Physically Fit	N
Generous	U
Humorous	U

b
Students' own answers.

4
What subjects they taught: *all subjects*
What this teacher looked like: *average height, thin, grey hair, a bun*
What kind of person they were: *quick and precise; a 'yes or no' kind of person*
How this person influenced you: *she taught me how to be firm but kind*

Script
<u>I can remember</u> a teacher called Miss Nicholls <u>really well</u>. She was a teacher I had when I was about six years old. She taught *all subjects*, not anything in particular. <u>Physically, she was</u> quite ordinary: she was about *average height*, *thin*, and with *grey hair in a bun*. She looked how you would expect for a person of her age – I would say she was about 50 years old. <u>Character-wise, she was</u> *quick and precise.* She was quick in all her movements, walking and speaking.

Answer Key

And she spoke very precisely. She was *a 'yes or no' kind of person*. Of course, before I moved into her class I was terrified of her. Now, many people have a rough exterior and a soft inside, but the extraordinary thing about Miss Nicholls was that she really did have a heart of gold. I'm sure <u>I'll never forget her because she taught me how to be firm but kind</u>.

5

a The … I've chosen is … ; I can remember … really well.
b I'll never forget him/her because …; What … taught me was that …
c He/she looked … ; Physically, he/she was …
d Character-wise, he/she was …; In terms of personality, …

6

I can remember … really well.
Physically, she was …
Character-wise, she was …
I'll never forget her because …

7

Students' own answers.

Making notes

1

physical: short, fat
psychological: amusing, relaxed
habits: looked out of the window while speaking, rolled tie up and down
why good teacher?: made boring subjects interesting, made difficult subjects easy
special quality: cheerful personality

2

a List A
b linear note-taking
c Students' own answers.

3

Students' own answers.

Pronunciation: placing stress in compound nouns

1

'article
a'ssistant
'journal
'tutor
regi'stration
'library
'lecturer
se'curity
'seminar

2

Column 1: Two words, one main stress	Column 2: Two words, two stresses
law tutor	young tutor
physics lecturer	amusing lecturer
journal article	difficult article
lab assistant	helpful assistant
registration day	beautiful day
security staff	polite staff
newspaper library	large library

3

Column 1 has the compound nouns. The main stress is in the first word of the compound noun. The words in the other column have stresses in the normal place. The rules are:
a In <u>compound nouns</u> the main stress is on the first word.
b In <u>other combinations</u> there is a stress on each word.

4

1 lecture theatre
2 revision class
3 seminar room
4 library card
5 help desk

Script

Jack Where are you going? To the *lecture theatre*?
Georgina No, a *revision class*. It's in *seminar room* number six.
Jack Oh right. Hope it's useful. I've lost my *library card*. I'm going to the *help desk* to see if I can get a new one.
Georgina Good luck. See you later.

Exam listening

Questions 31–35

31 B: … *seven weeks of term time plus two weeks of vacation.*
32 B: …*the very long summer holiday would be reduced in length.*
33 B: *On average, children's test scores were three weeks lower than when they left school …*
34 B: … *disadvantaged children showed even greater losses in reading skills.*
35 A: *This is certainly an improvement on the traditional system …*

Script

Lecturer So, having seen that the six-term system has passed the test of cost-effectiveness, we can move on to the educational aspects of this arrangement. Firstly, all the terms would be approximately the same length. Instead of terms of up to thirteen weeks, which we have now, there could be a repeating pattern of *seven weeks* of term time plus two weeks of vacation. This would be repeated six times per year. How does this affect the effectiveness of the educational provision? The most noticeable result would be that the very long summer holiday would be *reduced in length*. This by-product of the six-term system could be beneficial. There is plenty of evidence of huge learning loss by pupils during the summer holidays. By learning loss, we mean the amount that pupils forget – or lose – during a holiday break. Ashley carried out a number of analyses which showed this conclusively. He investigated 39 studies examining the effects of summer holidays on standardized test scores. His analyses indicated that summer learning loss equalled two weeks to seven weeks of instruction. On average, children's test scores were *three weeks* lower than when they left school in the previous term. He also found differences in the learning-loss effect according to subject. The subjects he analysed were reading, writing and maths, and he found that the effect was greatest in maths and reading. Furthermore, although all social groups experienced roughly similar learning-loss in the field of maths, the studies found that disadvantaged children showed even greater losses in *reading* skills. So the problem of learning-loss in traditional schools is clear. However, the results of studies into the six-term system and learning loss are ambiguous. Marchmont found that pupils in six-term schools maintained their test scores after the shorter holiday period. This is certainly an *improvement on the traditional system* where, as we have seen, pupils perform worse after the summer break. Benson, however, found no differences between those in traditional schools and on the six-term schedule. It would seem reasonable that if long holidays result in learning-loss, then shorter holidays should result in less learning-loss. So we await the outcome of further studies. Historically, of course, everyone knows the reason for our system of three terms per year. In days when *agriculture* was of much greater importance in our working lives, it was essential that the children helped with the harvest. Later on this changed and more people moved into the towns, but then there was a new problem. Before *air-conditioning*, it was very impractical to try to teach children in the summer months. Nowadays, that's no longer a barrier. One way of providing something different is the *summer school*. Here there is a completely different kind of educational provision. Cooper and others investigated 93 summer schools and the results they achieved. They all had a positive effect on learning. Most summer schools, of course, have small classes and *class size* was shown to have a positive effect. Additionally, summer school children usually benefit from a great deal of *parental support* – not least because payment of fees is involved – and this, as so often, was shown to produce very good outcomes. Results were most impressive in maths in general.

Questions 36–40
36 agriculture: *In days when agriculture was of much greater importance …*
37 air-conditioning: *Before air-conditioning, it was very impractical to try to teach children in the summer …*
38 summer school: *One way of providing something different is the summer school.*
39 class size: *Most summer schools … have small classes and class size was shown to have a positive effect.*
40 parental support: *… summer school children usually benefit from a great deal of parental support …*

Unit 5

Topic talk

1

Possible answers

a It is important for a youth worker to be articulate so that they can communicate effectively with young people. Being full of energy is an asset as the job can be tiring, as is being highly-motivated. Being experienced would help the youth worker to relate to a youth's situation. Being responsible is a suitable attribute as the youth worker will know what boundaries to set between him/herself and the young people they are working with. Being prepared to learn is perhaps less important.

b It would probably suit a younger person more, though an older person could also be suitable. Most young people would relate more to someone closer to their age. However, an older person would bring experience.
c Students' own answers.

2
2 f   6 i
3 h   7 e
4 a   8 d
5 b   9 g

3
a approachable
b well-mannered
c smart
d trustworthy
e educated
f smart
g accomplished
h adult
i lively

4
a unfriendly
b inarticulate
c scruffy
d careless
e uneducated
f slow
g inexperienced
h childish
i apathetic

5
Closed a, d
Open b, c, e, f, g, h

6
a Part 3
b Part 3
c Part 3
d Part 1
e Part 3
f Part 3
g Part 3
h Part 1 or Part 3

7
c There are many problems, but perhaps the greatest challenge is …
e The most likely development is that …
f By far the best way to tackle the situation is … because …
g The main difference is …

8
Students' own answers.

Listening skills Understanding maps

1
a the post office
b the shopping mall
c the shopping mall

2
1 b, d
2 c, f
3 d, f
4 d, e
5 a, e
6 c

3
1 c
2 a
3 b

4
a It is beside the food tent/near the food tent.
b It is between campsite 1 and the disabled viewing.
c It is between the stage and the bar.
d It is near the disabled viewing.

5
1 D   3 B
2 E

Script
Manageress Good morning everybody. I'd like to welcome you to the festival. My name is Sandy and I'm the general manager of Castle Music Events and I just want to take a moment to mention a few things to you before you go and have your detailed briefings in your work groups. You all have a copy of the plan of the festival grounds. Now most things are obvious, but I'd like to point out first the visitor toilets here along the side of the main area. Kindly do not use these yourselves – your own facilities, the staff toilets, are beside the food tent. Also, there are public telephones behind the stage. I mention these two things because they are places that visitors often ask for. For yourselves, one of the most important places is the staff meeting point. This is new this year and the only thing to remember is that it exists and that when you refer to a meeting point between yourselves you need to make clear which one you are talking about. The staff meeting point is between Campsite 1 and the disabled viewing area. This is not marked on the general maps but it is marked on the maps you've got there. The visitors' meeting point is, as you can see, in the centre of the main area, between the food tent and the entrance. Now another important facility is the first aid tent. This is a big round tent so you can't miss it. It's on the right-hand side of the entrance – again, as you come in. There are

many other first aid facilities all over the festival site. In fact, there is a first aid box in every tent and sales point, but this is the central point. Finally, I wanted to mention the security on the site. Every year the festival gets bigger and bigger and so every year we have to increase the security arrangements. We have a number of small security offices, one being near the entrance, but the main security office is opposite the disabled viewing area – it's next to the bar so that the officers can keep an eye on what's going on there. And of course, in that office there is a full supply of first aid equipment, too. And don't forget, those of you who can't wait till you get your pay at the end of the festival there are some cash machines in the wall of the bar.

Answering sentence and table completion questions

1
a the history of the festival
b 4 is an event; 5 is a thing; 6 is a place
c You can sometimes predict the *kind* of thing in the answer; sometimes, with numbers, the possible *range* of the numbers. The clock times are to some extent predictable, because they must be reasonable in the context of organizing a music festival.

2
4 pop concert
5 castle
6 fields
7 3.15
8 entrance gates
9 8
10 Campsite 1

Script
Manageress I do hope you'll enjoy working with us this year. It's always good to see some of last year's faces back with us again. We hope this year to put on an even better festival than before. The first year we put on a festival we called it the Mountain View Pop Concert. And it was a *pop concert* rather than a festival. We held it inside the castle and you could see the mountains in the background. It was very small and personal. Then we held it in front of the castle, with the *castle* in the background and then we started calling it the Castle Festival. Now, this year we have moved further away into the *fields*. The advantage is that the castle and the mountains are both there in the distance, but we have as much space as we want in the fields. The only problem with the fields is that sheep use the fields during the spring months and they leave little messages for us all over the place. So please be careful and encourage the visitors to be careful, too. Now it just remains for me to let you know the times of your detailed briefings which are as follows. And I'm telling you these as they are not – I repeat not – as written down on your welcome letters. Those of you who are working on the Children's Zone, your meeting is at 2 p.m. in Campsite 2. Those of you on the security team need to meet behind the stage at *3.15* p.m. For the people on first aid, please do not meet in the first aid tent – there will not be enough room – but meet at the *entrance gates* at 4 p.m. Finally, we need everybody, and I do mean everybody, on duty on Monday morning at *8* a.m. for the final clean-up. I'd like to remind you that Monday is the final day of work, not the Sunday. People not coming to the final day will lose 50 per cent of their pay. The meeting place for that is *Campsite 1*. Now, good luck and let's make this the best festival ever!

Speaking skills Describing jobs

1
Possible answers
a These are jobs, not careers.
b A career is long-term, perhaps with promotion and personal development.
c All of them are suitable for a student.
d Students' own answers.
e Students' own answers.

2
Possible answers
Pay
1 pop star
2 dentist
3 shop assistant
4 bus driver

Social usefulness
1 dentist
2 bus driver
3 shop assistant
4 pop star

3
Students' own answers.

4
Possible answers
architect: high job satisfaction, long training, social usefulness
nurse: long training, social usefulness
company director: high pay, variety of job activities, good pension
politician: variety of job activities, risk, high pay
doctor: expensive training, long training, social prestige, social usefulness, good pension, high job satisfaction, high pay
schoolteacher: long holidays, high job satisfaction, social usefulness
chef: high job satisfaction
footballer: social prestige, high pay, excitement, risk

Stating advantages and disadvantages

1
a Speakers 1 and 3
b Speaker 2
c Speakers 1 and 3

Script
Speaker 1 There are *pros and cons* with taking a job while studying. *On the one hand*, you earn money, which is useful. *On the other*, the job interferes with your study, which is a disadvantage. *On balance*, I'd prefer not to do a job, but I have to.

Speaker 2 I've been a nurse for twenty years. *The disadvantage with* nursing *is that* it is hard work and the pay is not great, but *the great advantage is that* I can choose my hours and work as many – or as few – as I want. So, *overall*, I'm happy to continue working.

Speaker 3 *The plus* is, of course, the wages you can earn, although students often don't earn a lot. Another advantage is the work experience, which sometimes can be very useful – meeting the right people and so on. *The minus* is the time you have to spend working instead of studying. *Weighing everything up*, I'd say 'Only work if you have to'.

2
a pros and cons
b On the one hand; On the other
c On balance
d The disadvantage with … is that
e the great advantage is that
f overall
g The plus
h The minus
i Weighing everything up

3

Possible answers

Travelling alone
a, b, c, g, h

Travelling with other people
d, e, f, i

4

Students' own answers.

5

Students' own answers.

Pronunciation: stressing compound adjectives

1

The university has a **well**-stocked library.
The library is **well**-stocked.

2

a The main stress is usually on the **first** part of a compound adjective, when it comes before a noun.

b The main stress is usually on the **second** part of a compound adjective, when it is alone, or after a verb.

3

easy-<u>go</u>ing
world-<u>fa</u>mous
<u>thou</u>sand-word
<u>end</u>-of-year
<u>cam</u>pus-based
<u>us</u>er-friendly
densely-<u>po</u>pulated
worry-<u>free</u>
<u>hour</u>-long

Script

I like it here. The tutors are open-**min**ded and easy-**go**ing. One or two of them are world-**fa**mous. I have to do a **thou**sand-word essay every fortnight and there is an **end**-of-year exam. The **cam**pus-based accommodation is very good, although it's not cheap. Internet connection is provided, and there's a **u**ser-friendly student intranet. The town is densely-**po**pulated and has lots of nightlife. Life is worry-**free** here. I must go now — I've got an **hour**-long seminar to prepare for.

4

Students' own answers.

5

Students' own answers.

Exam listening

Questions 1–3

1 G
2 F
3 D

Script

Accommodation officer Well, you have left things a bit late. Have you tried looking for somewhere in Newbridge?

Student Newbridge? No, I haven't. I've never heard of Newbridge.

Officer Well, let me show you – I've got a map here. Here's where everything is. You come into Newbridge over the bridge and the main road in front of you is, surprisingly enough, the High Street. This is one of the main streets.

Student Mmm …

Officer And branching off to the left, you can see there, is West Street – that is another busy part of town.

Student I see.

Officer Now, as I was saying, here is the High Street and here is West Street going left. Now if you go along West Street, the first place you come to on your right is the supermarket – it's not a very big one but it's got most things you're likely to need. Next to it, there's the old *town hall* – I say the old town hall because it is about a hundred years old, but it will soon make way for a car park, I'm afraid. I suppose the car is king. Now, opposite the supermarket is the *railway station*. You can get very frequent buses and trains from here in to the university. And next to that is the sports centre – it's a brand new one and was built on the site of some tennis courts, so that's progress. It's got everything the keen sportsperson like yourself might require. Now that's the centre of town and I want to point out to you the buildings opposite the supermarket, but on the other side of London Road. There are two buildings there: the one further away from the High Street is called The Heights and the one nearer the High Street is called *The Towers*.

Student What are they?

Officer They are where you could find a flat. One of them – The Heights – has a number of flats for rent at the moment.

Student Oh good.

Questions 4–8

4 A: *… apply to The Newbridge Accommodation Agency …*
5 C: *… you can ring the owner directly …*
6 B: *Leave it with me and I'll look into it for you …*
7 C: *… I suggest you just answer the advert here in the newspaper which the owner has obviously put in.*
8 A: *… I would have to advise you to go through the agency …*

Questions 9 and 10

9 clothing factories: *They were clothing factories and everyone worked in them …*
10 housing estates: *There are new housing estates on the edge of the town but they are mostly occupied by young families, and there isn't much student accommodation there.*

Script

Officer Now the first one is Flat 4. That's a nice flat with a balcony and you need to apply to *The Newbridge Accommodation Agency* to ask about that one. You'll find their number in the phone book. Number 6 is another nice one which has been empty for a while and *you can ring the owner directly*, I think … yes, I've got her number written here – there it is.

Student Right, thank you.

Officer Good. Now, number 8 is a re-advertisement –

Student What do you mean?

Officer Well, it did have a tenant, but now it is for rent again, so I'd like to ask about that one. *Leave it with me and I'll look into it for you*, then we can talk about it when I've got more information.

Student OK … are there others in this block?

Officer Yes, there's number 10, now this one's a bit strange. It's advertised with an agency as well as privately in the local paper. Normally, if it's advertised through an agency, you shouldn't really go behind the agency and go directly to the owner, but on this occasion *I suggest you just answer the advert here in the newspaper which the owner has obviously put in.*

Student OK.

Officer Finally, there is number 14. This is with the Newstart Agency – this is an agency started by the girl who was my assistant here and she left to make money for herself, so she's not my favourite person, but I'm afraid *I would have to advise you to go through the agency anyway*. Again, their number is in the phone book. All right, is that something for you to be starting with?

Student That's great. But what kind of place is Newbridge?

Officer It's a nice place. It was developed about a hundred years ago, really for people who worked in the factories around there. They were *clothing factories* and everyone worked in them – men, women, boys and girls. Then

… when the factories closed down things got very difficult for the town – there was a huge amount of unemployment, until a few years ago when, in the telecoms boom, a company making mobile phones started up – I think your phone was made in Newbridge – and now this company employs most of the people in the town. *There are new housing estates on the edge of the town but they are mostly occupied by young families, and there isn't much student accommodation there.* Most flats and so on are in the centre.
Student That sounds good.
Officer Well, let me know how you get on.
Student Yes, of course. Thank you. Bye.
Officer Bye.

Unit 6

Topic talk

1

a **Possible answer** The culture of a country is clearly reflected in its buildings and architecture. Otherwise, buildings would be the same throughout the world.
b **Possible answer** It is very important, because they are part of each country's heritage. Moreover, they are a source of tourist revenue.
c Students' own answers.
d **Possible answer** Traditional buildings can have modern additions, or, if they are of special interest, they can be renovated with modern interiors.

2

a How popular are modern buildings in your country?
b Is the architecture here the same as in your home country?
c Do you prefer traditional or modern architecture?/Do you prefer modern or traditional architecture?
d Is there any kind of building which you don't like?
e Do you have any buildings of special significance in your country?
f Has the type of building changed since you were a child?
g What kinds of building appeal to you most?

3

1 d	5 g
2 e	6 f
3 c	7 a
4 b	

4

1 c	5 g
2 e	6 f
3 d	7 a
4 b	

5
Students' own answers.

6

a dislike/hate
b would rather
c prefer
d stand
e appeal
f adore
g dislike/hate

7

Possible answers

a I much prefer reading contemporary books to classic literature.
b Plays in the theatre appeal to me more than outdoor drama.
c I am fond of watching films at home, but I have to say that I prefer films in the cinema.
d I would rather experience urban living than country life.
e I adore popular music, but I don't mind classical either.
f I can't stand keeping a diary, except for writing a blog.
g I don't hate art films. I just prefer Hollywood blockbusters.

Listening skills Understanding layout

1

a Layout B is easier to follow.
b Bold in title; italic type in subheadings; indentation for detailed information; lettering for the first list of points; capitals for subsection of *survey type*; underlining to emphasize *relative*; headings and titles for organization.

2

Possible answers

Fiji
Name of country Fiji
Capital Suva
Population 800,000
Ethnic composition
a Fijian
b Asian Indian
Climate hot and wet
Official language English
Crops
• 1 sugar
• 2 coconuts
Resources gold

Answer Key

Understanding noun phrases

1

a a cost-effective action plan
b a family shopping survey
c a celebrity gossip magazine
d a holiday price comparison website
e a child poverty report
f a television drama newspaper review

2

The order is reversed:
In description: 1. plan 2. action 3. cost-effective
In noun phrase: 1. cost-effective 2. action 3. plan
This reversal happens frequently, but not always.

3

b survey data collection
c exam preparation timetable
d Leeds University engineering student
e grammar reference book
f global warming news item

Predicting from notes

1

a Culture and Society
b Six
c Study, Sample, Questionnaire, Three examples of statements, Three examples of results, General conclusion
d With a final recommendation for further study
e The following are to some extent predictable: 1 is the name of something; 2 is a number, the size of the sample; 3 is a number; 4 is perhaps an abstract noun; 5 is a concrete noun, perhaps plural; 6 is the name of something; 7, 8, and 9 are nationalities; 10 is perhaps a word like *proved, confirmed, supported, contradicted, negated, rejected* or *refuted*.

2

1 materialism
2 556
3 7/seven
4 money
5 expensive things
6 possessions
7 Japanese
8 American
9 Chinese
10 not supported

Script

Lecturer Having referred briefly to the general definition of culture, I want to move on to an example of cultural research in action – a real example

101

of what researchers into culture are doing. This is a study done in 2004 into the 'global teenager hypothesis'. Now the global teenager hypothesis states that the values and attitudes of teenagers all over the world have become very similar, that teenagers are part of a global culture, rather than a national or a regional one. This study investigated the subject of *materialism* in three different cultures. It asked if teenagers' attitudes to materialism were similar or different in those three cultures. I'd like to go through the main points of this study because I think it demonstrates the interest and usefulness of this kind of research. The research took a sample of *556* high school students of between fourteen and seventeen years of age from three countries. The three countries – being also three differing cultures – were China, Japan and the USA. The high schools were in medium-sized cities and the students came from middle-class areas. There were 172 respondents from China, 168 from Japan and 216 from the USA. The students were asked to reply to a *seven*-statement questionnaire. They were asked to say if they agreed or disagreed with the statements. The questionnaire was filled in during the students' regular class time. I'll give you some examples of the statements in the questionnaire. And by the way, if you want to look into this in further detail – I've got the reference here, let me see, oh yes, it's *The International Journal of Consumer Studies*, Volume 28, Number 4, of September 2004. The first statement was: it's really true that *money* can make you happy. Respondents were asked – as they were asked about all the statements – to give their answer on a scale of one to seven. One on the scale indicated 'I strongly disagree'; four on the scale was neutral and seven on the scale was 'I strongly agree'. The second statement was: my dream in life is to be able to own *expensive things*. And the fifth was: having the right *possessions* is the most important thing in life. Let's look at some of the results. With regard to the first statement, it was the *Japanese* teenagers who agreed most strongly that money could make you happy. The *Americans* were second and the *Chinese* agreed least. However,

regarding one's life dream being to own expensive things, it was *American* teenagers who agreed most strongly with this and the Chinese who agreed least. As regards the fifth statement – about owning the right things – the Americans agreed less strongly than the other two groups. It was the *Chinese* who agreed most strongly with this statement. I haven't been able to analyse all aspects of the study in this lecture, but it does suggest that the hypothesis is not supported by the data. It may be that the culture of the USA is more individualistic, whereas the Chinese culture is more collectivist or communitarian. However, it *does not seem to support* the global teenager hypothesis. As always, this is something on which we need to carry out more research.

Speaking skills Talking about free time activities

1
a The first diary is an appointments diary, written in advance. The second is a record of events, written afterwards.
b The film was better because the diary says so. Apart from that, we cannot be sure.
c Students' own answers.
d Students' own answers.

2
1 golf, ice hockey, tennis, football
2 stamp-collecting, gardening, chess, going to concerts
3 meeting friends, going to parties, chatting on the phone, shopping, going to concerts

3
Students' own answers.

Expressing preferences

1
Speaker 1: listening to music, going to the cinema, going to the theatre (favourite).
Speaker 2: being outdoors, gardening, growing vegetables (favourite)
Speaker 3: sports, rugby (favourite)

Script
1
Interviewer What do you like doing in your free time, Charlotte?
Charlotte <u>I like</u> *listening to music* and *going to the cinema*, but <u>my favourite thing of all is</u> *going to the theatre*.
Interviewer Why do you like that best?
Charlotte <u>What attracts me most is that</u> it's live. It's that these people have come to this place, on this day to perform for us. <u>That's the great thing about</u> theatre.

2
Interviewer What do you like doing in your free time, Deborah?
Deborah <u>I enjoy</u> *being outdoors*, but <u>best of all, I like</u> *gardening*.
Interviewer Gardening?
Deborah Yes. <u>One thing I like about gardening is that</u> I can do it at home. <u>And the other thing is that I can</u> give a lot, or a little time to it. Also, <u>I can do it for fun or competitively</u> – the thing I like most is *growing vegetables* and entering them in competitions. But some years, I only have a little time and then I do it for fun, for enjoyment only.

3
Interviewer What do you like doing in your free time, Edward?
Edward <u>I like</u> *sports* in *general*. I find them relaxing. Best of all, I like *rugby*.
Interviewer You find rugby relaxing?
Edward Yes, <u>I really find it relaxing.</u> You see, I work very hard all week at a desk in an office, and in my free time I like doing something completely different.

2

Expressing preferences
I like listening to music.
My favourite thing of all is going to the theatre.
I enjoy being outdoors.
Best of all, I like gardening.
I like sports in general.

Explaining preferences
What attracts me most is that …
That's the great thing about …
One thing I like about gardening is that …
And the other thing is that I can …
I can do it for fun or competitively.
I really find it relaxing.

3
Students' own answers.

Dealing with unfamiliar topics

1
Students' own answers.

2
1 d 3 a
2 c 4 b

3
a The speaker knows little or nothing about the topic in the question.
b I'm afraid I have absolutely no skill in this area; I don't normally play games; Unfortunately not; I wish I could

Answer Key

c

Content of answer	Answer
Past experience and the result	c, d
No past experience and the reason	b
A reference to future intentions and hopes	a
A reference to personal level of skill	c, d

4
Students' own answers.

5
Students' own answers.

Pronunciation: shifting syllable stress

1
phil<u>o</u>sophy   ge<u>o</u>grapher   bi<u>o</u>logical

2

Subject	Person	adjective
ge<u>o</u>graphy	ge<u>o</u>grapher	geogr<u>a</u>phical
bi<u>o</u>logy	bi<u>o</u>logist	biol<u>o</u>gical
phil<u>o</u>sophy	phil<u>o</u>sopher	philos<u>o</u>phical

3

Subject	Person	adjective
p<u>o</u>litics	pol<u>i</u>tician	pol<u>i</u>tical
h<u>i</u>story	hist<u>o</u>rian	hist<u>o</u>rical

4
1 psychology   4 psychologists
2 biological   5 Biology
3 psychology

Exam listening

Questions 21–26

21 C: ... *investigate television but not what's happened in the past*
   ... *the emphasis must be on the future development of television* ...
22 B: *Screen size is the obvious way* ...
23 B: ... *just mini-programmes, say, four to five minutes long.*
24 B: ... *the Media Studies section will be closed for a week*...
25 A: *Denis Let's try the Premises committee*
   Tutor Good idea – why not?
   Emily OK.
26 C: ... *they'll send those copies directly to me.*

Script
Tutor Come in, sit down. Good to see you.
Denis, Emily Hello.
Tutor Now, this assignment, the best thing we can do, I think, is to think how we can approach it. The main point is to *investigate television, but not what's happened in the past*.
Emily I was thinking that it would be necessary to go over the new media first and then ...
Tutor Yes, that's a way to make a start, but you need to do that quite briefly ...
Emily But it's quite a complex topic ...
Tutor I agree, but *the emphasis must be on the future development of television* as a cultural phenomenon.
Emily Yes. I've been reading the talk by Ashley Highfield.
Tutor All right, and what do you take from that, what are the things that are competing with television?
Emily Well, obviously the personal computer and the Internet, but also the smartphone. And with the smartphone, there is the use of social media which television does not deal with at all.
Tutor Good, now, what's the problem with television in this new age?
Emily Well, first, television does not deal with the social media in any way, obviously. And it has fixed schedules for viewing ...
Tutor ... although this is changing ...
Emily ... yes. And, of course, people just love their smartphones!
Tutor Of course. But is there any way in which television has the advantage over these other things?
Emily *Screen size is the obvious way* – television was made for the size of screen it has, smartphones were not made to show action movies! Much more flexible schedules will be an improvement, but it seems that shopping and social contacts will stay with the smartphone.
Tutor Yes, I think you're right. You need always to look to the future and try to assess how things will develop. Good. Having said that, you need to move on to the newer social trends that we are seeing with television.
Emily Is one of them the idea that programmes might become shorter and shorter?
Denis Ah, yes, the average programme might be ten minutes or ...
Tutor ... or even less, *just mini-programmes, say, four to five minutes long*. Now, do you think you can get access to all the materials you need?
Denis The problem at the moment is the library.
Tutor Oh yes. What's happening there?
Denis There's a tremendous amount of noise because of the new extension they are building. It's quite impossible to work there.
Tutor They are stopping work for a week next week, I believe, and then all the sections will be open. There's a hold-up because some roof tiles have not arrived, so there will be peace for that week.
Emily But then after that *the Media Studies section will be closed for a week*, and all the noise and dirt will start up again.
Tutor Yes. But the Sociology section will be open and there's some good stuff there for you on this topic and it's further away from the noise.
Denis Yes, I don't think the Sociology section is affected at all and neither is the Journals section.
Tutor No, obviously they are rotating the closures and it was Sociology's turn to close for a week last term.
Denis I think we should make a complaint.
Tutor Yes, I think you should.
Denis I've had a word with the library staff – they are very sympathetic, but ...
Emily They are affected by these works just as we are.
Tutor If I were you I'd make a complaint directly to the Premises Committee. They only meet once a year but in fact I know they are having a meeting next Tuesday. You might like to make contact with them, but don't say I suggested this.
Emily Yes ... but the Students' Union might be better, since they are independent of the University.
Denis That's true, but I can't imagine that people haven't already approached them about this. *Let's try the Premises Committee.*
Tutor *Good idea – why not?*
Emily *OK.*
Tutor Now don't forget I need a copy of your dissertations by email and two copies in print, that is, on paper. If you give the reprographics office 24 hours' notice they'll make copies for you, and if you give them my details *they'll send those copies directly to me.* They won't send copies to you, so you'll need to take your own copy personally from them. Good. Any questions?

Questions 27–30

27 amateur video production/video material: *Amateur video production is a major challenge, for television – and for the Internet itself.*

103

28 Culture and Society
29 the University Theatre
30 4 July

Script

Emily One little thing was just that I wondered whether we should actually talk about the explosion of video material that is now being uploaded to the web, you know, to YouTube and also the social media websites.

Tutor I was rather hoping you hadn't overlooked that. Good point. *Video material* provides competition for television programmes, especially shorter ones of the kind we were talking about. *Amateur video production* is a major challenge, for television – and for the Internet itself. Anything else?

Denis Yes, I've got a question, I'm afraid. I'm not completely clear about the exact meaning of culture, as we're using it in this subject.

Tutor Well, Mrs Jones is giving a lecture on *Culture and Society* in *the University Theatre*. It's on Wednesday at 10 a.m. and you can learn all about it there, I am sure.

Denis Can you give us that again, please?

Tutor Yes. That's Culture and Society. It's in the University Theatre. And let me just check the time, yes, here it is, 10 a.m. on Wednesday. She'll be giving a very thorough discussion of the issues in defining what culture means.

Denis Right. That's good. The thing is, the reading list confused me a bit. One thing that occurred to me was that it might be broken down into subsections for future students.

Tutor Yes, that's a fair point. I'll bear that in mind. Now don't forget, you need to do the reading, and finish the assignment by the *4th July*. Is that OK?

Emily Fine. Thank you very much.

Unit 7

Topic talk

1
Students' own answers.

2

a **Possible answer**
I think some people are naturally inclined to the arts or sciences, but the environment also plays a part. For example, it is difficult to imagine scientists playing the roles that some actors play, and vice versa.

b Students' own answers.

c Students' own answers.
d Students' own answers.

3
b accomplished
c rigorous
d original
e talented
f expressive
g impartial
h creative
i curious

4
b accomplishment
c rigour
d originality
e talent
f expressiveness
g impartiality
h creativity
i curiosity

5

Possible answer
Someone who is involved in the arts has to have talent, because it is not easy to entertain people if one doesn't have a special gift for doing so. For example, it is not everyone who can stand on a stage and sing a song or make people laugh.

6
a hall of residence regulations
b examination rules and regulations
c assignment guidelines
d assessment criteria
e society/club constitution
f set of instructions
g assignment deadline
h application

7
Students' own answers.

8
not optional   requisite
mandatory   imperative
obligatory

9

Possible answers
a It is essential in order to gain good marks and to help prepare for work in later life. Assignments help prepare people for independent work in the real world.
b Visuals help to illustrate ideas. Because a picture says more than a thousand words, they are desirable but not essential, especially if one is a good speaker.
c A bibliography shows which materials, such as books and journals, have been looked at as sources. This is important because other people can then follow up the ideas elsewhere if they want to.

d Preparation is vital because it reduces the amount of work later on. What's more, in order to illustrate one's approach it is essential to have many ideas, facts and figures to hand. For example, it would be difficult to write about a historical event without knowing the background facts.
e At least one draft is strongly advisable, if not essential. In order to refine one's ideas, it is sometimes necessary to rewrite something three or four times.
f The key to preparing a good assignment is addressing the whole question, since it is easy to overlook an important part of the task.
g In order for a lecturer and fellow students to follow what is being said, it is important to speak clearly and naturally. Organization is also a prerequisite, if fellow students are to extract information. Because technology is in every part of the curriculum, it is essential for students to be completely computer literate.

Listening skills Making questions from statements

1
a science; visits to a festival
b student teachers

2

Possible answers
2 How long should the student teachers arrange the visits to last?
3 What is the most important purpose of the festival visits?
4 What are the central features of our scientific age?

3
1 C: *… the head of science at your school will be aware of the festival and should have all the details of it …*
2 A: *We hope you will encourage your pupils to visit it on one or two days.*
3 B: *… we hope you will use the festival to generate a lively interest in science …*
4 A: *… we live in a truly scientific age, which means one where inventions and improvements are matters of routine …*
5 B: *… maths is being taught by biologists …*

Script

Lecturer Now, I think nearly all of you have received confirmation of your school placements for next term and, as part of your activities, we'll be asking you to take responsibility for promoting a school visit to the Norchester Science Festival. Of course, *the heads of science at your school will be aware of the festival and should have all the details of it,* but all the heads of science at your schools will be looking to you to be the main organizers and motivators of a visit to the festival. They'll give you the documents you need. We hope that you will motivate pupils at your schools to take an interest in the festival. It runs for three days. There are day tickets and special three-day tickets, and schools have the extra option of a two-day ticket. *We hope you will encourage your pupils to visit it on one or two days.* But, most important of all, *we hope you will use the festival to generate a lively interest in science* that will last all year round and provide the school with a lasting benefit. This will, with luck, lead to improved examination results in science subjects. And let's not forget – we hope your pupils will have a lot of fun, too. Needless to say, your performance in achieving these aims will count towards your final exam grade at the end of the year. Now, let me just say a few words on why a science festival. Science is part of our everyday world in a way that is different now from before. Of course, we are used to having the benefit of scientific inventions: we are used to the aeroplane, the motorcar, the space rocket and so on. But now *we live in a truly scientific age, which means one where inventions and improvements are matters of routine* rather than occasional and unusual events. We have become a really scientific society. Yet, we find that we are failing to interest and enthuse the young in this. Fewer young people are choosing to study science at school after the age of sixteen, and even fewer at university. As a result, we have fewer teachers coming into schools to teach science. And many science teachers are not teaching their specialism. For example, I know of several cases where *maths is being taught by biologists* and chemistry is being taught by physicists. We urgently need another 3,000 science teachers in England, at least. That's why we look to you, the science teachers who are starting off your careers, to inject enthusiasm and wonder into the study of science. And we hope the Norchester Festival will help you to do this.

Paraphrasing for matching

1
Chapter 1: c
Chapter 2: a
Chapter 3: e
Chapter 4: b
Chapter 5: d

2
a journey through the past centuries
b celebrated
c studying the stars
d innovations
e catastrophes

3
a types of events
b that these are titles of events
c the list A–E – it would not normally be possible to paraphrase the proper names and titles in the other list.
d **Possible answers**
a show:
a performance, an entertainment, an act
an event of local interest:
regional, a district, an area, interest, importance
a technical demonstration:
an explanation, an example, a working model
an open discussion:
a conversation, a round table, a debate, contributions
an interactive event:
all invited to join in, everyone takes part

4
6 B   9 E
7 D   10 C
8 A

Script
Lecturer Now, enough of the background, what about the festival? There are three main venues where the festival events take place. These are the Millennium Library, the town hall – not the town hall itself but the town hall Conference Centre – and the Norchester Theatre. When you're planning your visits, remember that many of the activities for younger pupils will be at the Millennium Library, and the secondary school pupils may find more to interest them in the Conference Centre. Now, just so that you have some immediate information, I'd like to mention a few of the events that are taking place this year. One event of special interest to people living in this area is called *Waterworld*. This is a clay model of the south-east of England and the presenters show you the effects of rising sea levels as a result of climate change. They ask the audience to select the rise in sea level, for example 20 or 40 or 60 centimetres, and the model shows the places that would be flooded as a result. Watch out for your town – does it sink or does it swim? *Transport 2050* is about transport options for our towns in the future. A number of experts will introduce the topic, and then everyone at the event will have a chance to speak and give their views. *Science in a suitcase* is a comedy act by two scientists who do crazy experiments and sing songs and play the clown to large audiences every afternoon. I'm particularly looking forward to that one, which should be entertaining. *Ropes and hangings* is an interactive event, which will be of interest to young people in which, after experimenting with ropes and bricks, they build a real suspension bridge. That kind of hands-on activity is always really popular. And, appealing to a different audience, there is *Paper and time,* in which some experts will be showing us the techniques they use for the conservation of ancient books and manuscripts. This will obviously not be for everybody, but it should be interesting just to see how they do it. Now, let's move on to tickets and transport to the festival.

Speaking skills Comparing and evaluating

1
a In the first case, the accident was the head becoming separated from the stand. In the second case, the accident was forgetting about the liquid.
b Students' own answers.

2
Possible answer
Arts
knowledge of humanity
performance
creative
mysterious
literacy
work of art
imagination
original
uncertainty

105

Sciences
numeracy
analytical
demonstration
discipline
knowledge of the universe
experiment
certainty
incremental
definite

3
Students' own answers.

4
a comparison
b evaluation
c evaluation
d comparison

5
1 a; d
2 b; c
3 c
4 d
5 a; d
6 d

6
Students' own answers.

Expressing others' views

1
Students' own answers.

2
Speaker 1: c
Speaker 2: a
Speaker 3: b

Script
Speaker 1 Well, <u>some people would say that</u> it's a great help, in that lots of tasks are much easier than they were in the past. <u>I'm not sure because</u> some gadgets create a lot of work in themselves to maintain. And we end up just finding other new chores to take up the time.

Speaker 2 <u>It's often said that</u> the arts offer something to society, and therefore it's in everyone's interests if they get funding from the state. <u>That's not my view, because,</u> if they were really that important, people would just be happy to pay higher ticket prices. Besides, if there was no funding, it would force them to think more commercially.

Speaker 3 <u>There is an argument that</u> scientists are too isolated: that they work in specialized departments and don't really think about the consequences of their ideas on the world outside. <u>I really don't think that's true</u>. I mean, things have changed, and a lot of scientists are interested in how their work is seen by non-specialists.

3
Speaker 1: a
Speaker 2: e
Speaker 3: f

4
Speaker 1: *Well, some people would say that …*
Speaker 2: *It's often said that …*
Speaker 3: *There is an argument that …*

5
Speaker 1: *I'm not sure because …*
Speaker 2: *That's not my view, because …*
Speaker 3: *I really don't think that's true.*

6
Students' own answers.

Pronunciation: weak forms and /ə/

1
<u>a</u>bout   Int<u>e</u>rnet   doct<u>o</u>r

2
a … <u>some</u> ultra-modern buildings …
b <u>There</u> is a university …
c … <u>that</u> you will find …

3

	/ə/ used for the vowel sound ✓/✗
Some meaning a part of a greater number	✗
Some meaning an indefinite amount	✓
There meaning a place	✗
There introducing a sentence	✓
That pointing at something	✗
That connecting two parts of a sentence	✓

4
The Mercury Gallery has opened an art exhibition in Bond Street. **There** are paintings by foreign and British artists **there**. You can see **some** examples of the best **that** modern art can offer. **Some** works are abstract and **some** are figurative, but all are wonderfully imaginative. **That** is why the exhibition is so popular.

5
Students' own answers.

Exam listening

Questions 21–25
21 350
22 access
23 everyone
24 value for money
25 recovery

Script
Briony What have you been working on, Arthur?
Arthur I've been looking into the funding of the arts by the Arts Association.
Briony Oh, Mr Simpson gave you that topic, did he?
Arthur Yes, it's not too difficult. At least all the facts and figures are easy to find, or I think they will be. I've done a lot of useful stuff already. Simpson hasn't asked me to present my research for the past few seminars, so I think he might ask me this time.
Briony Well, what have you found out?
Arthur Well, it's big money at the Arts Association. £*350* million from the government and £118 million from the Lottery. Let me see, I've got my notes here. Now, the Arts Association mission statement tells us that it exists to develop, sustain and promote the arts. So that's clear, but then we need to know exactly how it can do this. However, before we get to that, there are certain issues which the Association must take into account.
Briony What are those issues?
Arthur They are, first, *access*. This is the idea that the arts mustn't be just for the few.
Briony Not just Italian opera, but pop concerts, too?
Arthur Something like that. Other issues are education, cultural diversity, social regeneration and social inclusion. All these are different ways of saying that the arts are for *everyone*.
Briony All right, but what does it actually do?
Arthur It does what it wants, I think. The government doesn't interfere in its activities, but demands that it gets *value for money* for its funds.
Briony But there must be certain programmes that it carries out?
Arthur Oh yes. There is the touring programme, which is what it says, that is, a programme to support …
Briony … give money to …
Arthur … yes, that's right… to support touring companies, for example, dance companies, orchestras and

Answer Key

so on. There is also the *recovery programme*.

Briony What on earth is that?

Arthur It's a financial programme to give extra money to organizations which are financially in a bad way or which might have financial difficulties in the future. Like it says, it's for their recovery.

Briony It all seems very complicated.

Arthur It is.

Questions 26–30
26 D: *… Greenberg, who covers contemporary art and up-to-the-minute movements …*
27 A: *As far as the economic impact of art is concerned, a basic text is the Parliamentary report on art and the UK economy.*
28 F: *It's about the whole trade in art as a phenomenon.*
29 C: *… the relationship of art to the other aspects of culture, such as film, television, books, and so on.*
30 B: *It's sort of about how art relates to how we think.*

Script

Briony Did you get any information on the reading for the other half of our work?

Arthur Yes, I did. You mean the Art and Society module?

Briony Yes.

Arthur Yes. I met Simpson himself as we were waiting for a train at Norchester station so I managed to ask him.

Briony Any luck?

Arthur Yes. I've got the notes I took here. He told me, of course, to start with *Greenberg, who covers contemporary art and the up-to-the-minute movements* in America. It's about the modern movements really. *As far as the economic impact of art is concerned, a basic text is the Parliamentary report on art and the UK economy.* This gives lots of monetary facts and figures, but the figures are not very satisfactory as, of course, a lot of the information is confidential and can't be published. *Art Now! Art Wow!* by someone called Dennison sounds exciting and is about how art and artists are created, presented for buyers and sold in the US. *It's about the whole trade in art as a phenomenon.*

Briony Like a product, like washing powder …

Arthur Yes … . That's the idea of the book, anyway. And there's another one here, oh yes, by someone called Hampton. It's a book called *American Art* which Simpson says is full of discussion on *the relationship of art to the other aspects of culture, such as film, television, books and so on.*

Briony Popular culture, I suppose.

Arthur Not just popular … culture of all sorts, I imagine. Finally, for the spiritual and more abstract aspects of art, he recommends *Art and the Mind of Modern Man* by Frick. *It's sort of about how art relates to how we think.* He did have lots of other recommendations, but luckily his train arrived before he could move on to them. These seem enough to me.

Briony Yes. They're a good place to start. We will be busy.

Unit 8

Topic talk

1
a Students' own answers.
b **Possible answer**
Places like those in the picture appeal to people because they are idyllic and peaceful. They offer people tranquillity and the space to be themselves.
c **Possible answer**
The world is more and more stressful so we need places where we can escape from the problems of general living. People with stressful lives often like to retreat to places like this to relax and unwind. It is also good to think of such places when one is stressed.
d Students' own answers.

2
a enthusiastic
b enthusiastic
c enthusiastic
d unenthusiastic
e unenthusiastic
f unenthusiastic
g enthusiastic
h enthusiastic

3
Possible answers
b 2   f 3
c 1, 2, 4, 5   g 1, 2, 4, 5
d 5   h 2, 5
e 5

4
a What makes me feel so relaxed there is the silence.
b What does me a lot of good is being away from the city.
c What makes the place restful is the fact that there are no shops.
d What makes the sea clean is the fact that there are no factories.
e What makes the garden very private is the trees.
f What makes the area so welcoming is the people.
g What makes the area appealing is the many tourist attractions.

5
b Why does it do you a lot of good?
c Why is the place so restful?
d Why is the sea so clean?
e Why is the garden so private?
f Why is the area so welcoming?
g Why is the area so appealing?

6
Students' own answers.

7
Possible answers
b What I recollect most is its playfulness, especially when it was young.
c What I will always remember is the way it was wrapped.
d What made me feel so uncomfortable is the fact that there were so many people around.
e What made it so memorable is the friends that I made on the trip.
f What made the trip unforgettable is the number of places we managed to visit.

8
Students' own answers.

Listening skills Changing opinions

1
a Speakers B, C, E and G.
b Speaker B: *no, I mean …*
Speaker C: *… in fact.*
Speaker E: *Actually, you're right.*
Speaker G: *Yes, that's what I meant*

2
a 5
b 2
c the end

Answering multiple choice questions

1
animals, zoos (and museums) are all likely

2
Students' own answers

3

Questions 1–3
1 C: *We have to cover the history, but not in great depth.*
2 F: *Our main focus is the scientific aspects of zoos …*
3 E: *The other thing we should cover is the educational side of their work …*

107

Questions 4 and 5
4 C/D 5 C/D

Script

Adrian Hello Brenda, how are you doing?
Brenda Fine. I've just come over to talk about this assignment on the function of zoos. Oh, hello, Charles.
Charles Hello, Brenda. That's good. I've just been in the library looking at some stuff. I think Adrian's been on the web.
Adrian Yes, I have.
Brenda Well, that's great. What have you found out about zoos?
Charles I've been looking into the history, both of zoos and of keeping animals generally.
Adrian I didn't think we had to do that.
Brenda Yes, it was one of the topics we had to research. We definitely need to cover it, even if only briefly, I think. After all, people have kept animals for recreation and pleasure for centuries. The ancient Egyptians kept collections of animals, and of course the Romans kept animals for recreation.
Adrian Ah, the Romans. That brings us to the general question of the treatment of animals, and the mistreatment of them …
Charles Yes, but that's not our topic. We've been told to keep off that. Now, where were we?
Brenda Our assignment is concerned with the purposes of zoos in general, and in our modern era. *We have to cover the history, but not in great depth. Our main focus is the scientific aspects of zoos, and the work they do for conservation, and so on.*
Adrian We mustn't forget the question of who pays for them. Zoos are hugely expensive places to run nowadays. There are the costs of feeding the animals obviously, and security for the animals and the public, what happens if they escaped and so on. We have to ask what benefits we get from this.
Brenda Adrian, I don't think you'll find we have to do that kind of thing at all.
Adrian Oh. But I've been looking into all that, and the social benefits of zoos …
Brenda What I mean is, that's not part of this assignment. All this financial and safety stuff is not necessary. We should stick to their purposes. Now, what have you found out, Charles?
Charles Well, I discovered that the World Association of Zoos and Aquariums was very helpful on this. I've got their website address here somewhere. I found out about the scientific research that zoos do. *The other thing we should cover is the educational side of their work …*
Adrian The educational side is pretty obvious. I've got lots of stuff here about this and more references to websites and information. There's also the area of entertainment. What about that?
Charles He's got a point. I think we need to do some more research on that.
Brenda Fine. But it sounds like we've covered the history and science angles pretty well.
Charles I agree, *let's leave those for now and plan some more study on the entertainment stuff.*
Brenda *And let's do some more work on the conservation element.*

Completing a summary (2)

1
6 a colour
7 an adjective
8 a date
9 a number
10 an activity

2
6 white
7 hot (desert)
8 1972
9 300
10 illegal hunting

Script

Adrian Oh yes. The Arabian oryx is a classic case.
Brenda The what?
Adrian The Arabian oryx. It's like a deer, but *white*. That is, it has a white body but brown legs, and long curved horns. It normally lives in the *hot* desert in the Arabian peninsular. Anyway, in the 70s the population declined and in *1972* the last wild oryx was shot and it became extinct in the wild. There were a few left in zoos in the United States, where there was a captive breeding programme. This was so successful that in 1982 a small population was reintroduced into the wild. Hunting of wild animals was made illegal and there are now about *300* in Oman.
Charles Although there was a big problem there, I believe. The population went up to about 450 in the 90s and then *illegal hunting* did take place. The population crashed again and the programmes had to be restarted. But that's been successful and there are now, I believe, as you say, several hundred in the wild. This is all available on the websites that Adrian has noted.
Adrian Mmm. There was a similar programme in Saudi Arabia and I think there are hundreds there now.
Brenda We can use that as a definite success story.
Adrian And what have you found out?
Charles Yeah, what have you come up with?
Brenda I'm going to the library now.
Charles Good.

Speaking skills Describing animals

1
a dog
b cat
c horse

2
a dog: jump up, wag their tails, bark
b cat: arch their backs, scratch, curl up, purr
c horse: get excited, jump

3
a take them for walks, throw sticks for them
b let them curl up on one's lap, stroke them
c look after them, feed them, groom them

4
a The fondest memory I have is …
b But what I remember most is …
c What sticks in my mind is …

5
a Speaker 2
b Speaker 1
c Speaker 3

Script

Speaker 1 Yes I did, although in fact I wouldn't call him a pet, exactly. Rover was our guard dog, but he had a peculiar way of guarding the house. We had burglars twice and on each occasion he didn't bark or attack the burglars. He ran out of the house to the neighbours' house and barked at their front door. Both times they called the police and the burglars were caught. So in his way he was an excellent guard dog.
Speaker 2 Like most parrots, he was very colourful. I'm not really sure if a parrot is a real pet – they're not very friendly or affectionate. Anyway, he spoke very little, but when he did …!
Speaker 3 My favourite pet animal was Lassie. Of course, she wasn't my

Answer Key

pet at all, but I loved her. I had lots of books about her and, of course, I watched the television programmes whenever I could. I thought she was wonderful.

6
Speaker 1: … although in fact I wouldn't call him a pet, exactly.
Speaker 2: I'm not really sure if a parrot is a real pet …
Speaker 3: Of course, she wasn't my pet at all …

7
Students' own answers.

Describing presents
1
a **Possible answer**
Reminding people who are thinking of giving an animal as a present, that having an animal is a responsibility that lasts as long as the pet lives.
b Students' own answers.
c Students' own answers.

2
Students' own answers.

3
a *Present madness*
b Students' own answers.
c Students' own answers.

4
Students' own answers.

Pronunciation: contrastive stress
1
b We wanted an active d<u>o</u>g.
c We wanted him to bark at intr<u>u</u>ders.
d We wanted him to bite b<u>u</u>rglars.
e We wanted him to wake up at the sound of the al<u>a</u>rm.

2
The main or sentence stress is normally on the **last** content word in the sentence.

3
b We wanted him to bark at intruders, *but he l<u>i</u>cked intruders.*
c We wanted him to bite burglars, *but he w<u>e</u>lcomed burglars.*
d We wanted him to wake up at the sound of the alarm, *but he fell asl<u>ee</u>p at the sound of it.*

4 When there is a contrast of ideas, **the contrasting words** carry the main stress.

5 Students' own answers.

6 a & b
… firstly, the bell. It's one thing **to have a q<u>u</u>iet bell**, but this **was a wh<u>i</u>spering bell**. Then the light: at night one **needs**

a bright light, not like this one, which was **the f<u>ai</u>ntest of lights**. Then, it was heavy. I needed to take it on the train, so **a light bike was what I needed**. I sold it back to the shop and bought **a more exp<u>e</u>nsive bik**e, which I still have – **my dr<u>e</u>am bike**. But while **I h<u>a</u>d the bike …**

c Students' own answers.

Exam listening
Questions 31–33
31 A nesting: *It nests in trees and buildings …*
32 C feeding: *It feeds on insects and fruit.*
33 F global distribution: *Its native range includes the British Isles and Finland, but it is also found in most of Europe and parts of Asia and Africa.*

Questions 34–37
34 crops: *They gather in large flocks of thousands of birds and feed together on commercial crops.*
35 financial: *This causes great financial damage to farmers.*
36 mess: *… they also make a mess …*
37 diseases: *… starlings may carry diseases …*

Questions 38–40
38 C prevention: *The best approach of course is prevention …*
39 B the deposit and pick-up of water: *regulations on how and where ships may pick up and deposit water*
40 C politics: *The most important decision has to be made in the political forum …*

Script
Lecturer Thousands of exotic plants and animals have been introduced into the British Isles over thousands of years. These newcomers compete with native species for resources, and can also cause major changes in the wildlife and in the habitats of our countryside. The problem is not just British of course, but global, and it has been going on for centuries. One good example of this I'd like to mention today is the European starling. The starling, to us in the UK, is a fairly ordinary little bird, about eight inches long. In flight it appears to be black or grey with tiny white spots. So it's a very ordinary-looking, almost dirty-looking bird. *It nests in trees and buildings* and can be found in the country and in towns. It travels in large flocks, leaving the nests in the morning and returning in the early evening. *It feeds on insects and fruit. Its native range includes the British Isles and Finland, but it is also found in most of Europe and parts of Asia and Africa.* In the British Isles and Finland, however, it has suffered a huge decline, and in these countries there is an effort to conserve the species. It is a different story in some of the places where it has been introduced. For example, the population in the USA is estimated at 170 million birds. Also, they are becoming a big problem in Australia and New Zealand. Starlings, as I have said, nest in trees and it has been found that they are more aggressive than the native species when they are looking for nesting places. They therefore compete with native species for nests and also they drive those species away from nests. So, this nest-building activity causes harm to native species, but also they are a nuisance to humans. *They gather in large flocks of thousands of birds and feed together on commercial crops. This causes great financial damage to farmers.* And *they make a mess*, both in the town and the countryside. There is also the problem that *starlings may carry diseases* which affect both humans and other animals, although this has not been really confirmed and we are waiting for more work to be done on this. The question arises – what are we to do about foreign species which not only do damage to native species, but interfere with human activity? We have three approaches in theory, but usually it is not a free choice between them. Usually, we have to do the best we can and that money will allow. *The best approach of course is prevention*, and many countries have passed legislation which attempts to limit or prevent the arrival of non-native species in their countries. In particular, there are many international *regulations on how and where ships may pick up and deposit water*, and this is a major contribution to preventing the accidental transport of fish and organisms by ship, since accidental transport by ship is a frequent cause of fish and other creatures going from place to place. Ports also have special areas where water can be deposited, and many of them have treatment facilities to kill any foreign species that may establish themselves in their waters. For fish and organisms that live in water, these

international regulations are useful, but obviously not all species can be dealt with in this way. Sometimes, it is simply too late for prevention. Then we have to consider eradication or management. By management I mean that we have to decide how best to live with the new creatures and how to keep their numbers down. However, this becomes not only a scientific question. It can be a matter of choosing what population level of an invasive species we want to maintain. This choice involves costs: there is the cost of living with the species and there is the cost of managing the species over time (and species management is usually a long-term business without any foreseeable end). However, there is not just the economic aspect to this question. We can also consider the ethical point: how should we treat animals which we have, sometimes deliberately, introduced into the environment? Is it permissible just to exterminate a number of them convenient to ourselves? *The most important decision has to be made in the political forum*, no matter what considerations go into the making of that decision. These questions are relevant also to the approach of eradication, which is another option but which does not have an encouraging history. Many attempts have been made to eradicate introduced species …

Unit 9

Topic talk

1
a Students' own answers.
b **Possible answer**
   Cycling is more useful as it's something you can do easily every day to stay fit and healthy.
c Students' own answers.
d kitesurfing: adventure sports; outdoor sports; water sports
   BMX racing: outdoor sports
   snowboarding: adventure sports; other (winter sports)
   other sports: possible answers
   water sports: swimming; waterskiing; sailing; scuba-diving
   adventure sports: mountaineering; sky-diving
   motor sports: motorcycle racing; karting

blood sports: hunting; shooting
team sports: football; hockey; netball
non-contact sports: swimming; athletics
racket sports: badminton; tennis; squash
indoor sports: basketball; table tennis
outdoor sports: rugby; cricket

2
1 d   4 e
2 f   5 b
3 a   6 c

3
Students' own answers.

4
opponent
opportunity

5
Possible answers
a Doing sport can mean getting fewer illnesses.
b Doing exercise can help you learn new skills.
c Playing football can help you meet new people.
d Doing exercise makes you feel more relaxed.
e Certain sports can help you learn how to be part of a team.
f Doing sport gives you the opportunity to be in a competitive atmosphere.
g Doing sport gives you the opportunity to be outdoors.

6
Students' own choice of three.
a people get few illnesses
b people learn new skills
c you can meet new people
d people feel more relaxed
e you can be part of a team
f there's a competitive atmosphere
g there are opportunities to be outdoors

7
a people get few illnesses, people feel more relaxed, there are opportunities to be outdoors
b people learn new skills, there's a competitive atmosphere, there are opportunities to be outdoors
c you can meet new people, you can be part of a team, there's a competitive atmosphere

8
Students' own answers.

Listening skills Predicting in tables (2)

1
Possible answers
1 language difficulties
2 student debt
3 feeling homesick
4 examination pressure
5 poor accommodation
6 colds and flu

2
a **Possible answers**
   not liking the food, difficulty in making friends, not knowing where things are, finding the work difficult
b **Possible answers**
   feeling homesick
   – counselling service
   examination pressure
   – counselling service
   colds and flu
   – health centre
   poor accommodation
   – counselling service
   language difficulties
   – counselling service
   student debt
   – counselling service
c Students' own answers.

3
a You will hear the information from left to right, dealing with each student service in turn.
b 2, 4 and 5
c 1 is probably a geographical expression; 3 is possibly a compass direction, such as north, south, east or west.

4
1 yellow: *… there's a map at the centre which shows you the area that the university practice can accept people from – it's what we call the yellow zone.*
2 8/eight: *… it's free, but that's only for up to eight sessions.*
3 Central: *… the Nightline service, which is run from an office on the Central Campus.*
4 0900 7625913
5 22: *You have to present your student card and pay a fee of £22 to get a pass …*

Script
Student Hi. I wonder if you could help me. I'm starting a course at Glenfield in a few weeks. I was just a bit worried about what facilities there will be and what I'll have to do. I'm especially interested in health and welfare stuff.

110

Answer Key

Advisor Certainly. We normally send out a copy of our leaflet 'Staying healthy at Glenfield'. I'm not sure why you haven't had it.
Student Well, could you answer a few questions for me? Firstly, I'm wondering about how I get a doctor when I arrive.
Advisor Well, you can register with the University Health Centre on North Campus.
Student And do I have to pay for that?
Advisor Not to register, but if you have to get medicines, there's a prescription charge of £6.50.
Student OK. Well, I'm not planning to get ill. That's only going to arise if I have any problems. So should I just go along when I arrive?
Advisor That's what we recommend for peace of mind. But it's not compulsory, and if you don't live inside the catchment area, you can't in fact register there. Where do you live?
Student Well, at the moment I'm staying at the backpackers' hostel in Hill Street, but I will be moving from there shortly. Somewhere nearer.
Advisor Well, *there's a map at the centre which shows you the area that the university practice can accept people from – it's what we call the yellow zone.* If you live outside that area, you have to find another medical centre to register with.
Student It sounds like I'll only qualify after I move.
Advisor I think you might be right. Then, in addition to the Health Centre, there's a free Counselling service for all students situated on the North Campus. You don't have to register. They also have drop-in sessions. I say *it's free, but that's only for up to eight sessions.* Beyond that they normally refer people elsewhere.
Student Sounds serious.
Advisor Well, it's not just for big problems. People go there for advice on housing, workload, whatever really. They can even arrange financial help.
Student Is it confidential?
Advisor Absolutely. Then again, a lot of students prefer to phone *the Nightline service, which is run from an office on the Central Campus.* They don't really encourage people to drop in.
Student I see.
Advisor So it's basically a free phone line. The number, if you want to make a note, is *O – nine hundred – seven six two – five nine – one three*. I'll say it again. *O – nine hundred – seven six two – five nine – one three.*
Student Fine. Well I hope I won't need any of these. What I will want is access to some gym facilities.
Advisor Right. Well, you'll find those on the South Campus in the Sports Centre. It's great, but it's not free. *You have to present your student card and pay a fee of £22 to get a pass*, but that will last you for the whole year.

Spelling words

1 & 2
List 1 a, h, j, k
List 2 b, c, d, e, g, p, t, v
List 3 f, l, m, n, s, x, z
List 4 i, y
List 5 q, u, w

3
Message for: Susan
Message: send the birthday present to 18, Grosvenor Crescent, Southwark JG8 2AE
Caller's number: 01324 781205
Message from: Jane Smith
Time: 2.30 p.m.
Date: (Tuesday) 4th

Script
Answer machine I'm afraid I can't take your call at the moment. Please leave your message after the tone.
Caller Hello, erm, as nobody's there I'll leave a message. Erm, this is a message for *Susan*. Could you please *send the birthday present to* this address: *18 Grosvenor Crescent*, that's Grosvenor – G-R-O-S-V-E-N-O-R – Crescent, *Southwark*, that's S-O-U-T-H-W-A-R-K. The postcode is *JG8 2AE*. I hope that's clear. Any problems, please ring me on *01324 781205*. Oh, I should say this is *Jane Smith*, at around *2.30 p.m.* on *Tuesday the fourth*. Bye.

4
Students' own answers.

5
6 (whole) information pack
7 Sonia Orr
8 Winter Gardens
9 GF23
10 Economics (and) Sociology

Script
Student Is this information on the website?
Advisor I'm afraid not. I can send you some leaflets or even resend the *whole information pack*, if you give me your details.
Student Could you send the whole information pack please?
Advisor Yes, that's fine. I'll have to take down some details. Could you tell me your full name?
Student *Sonia Orr*.
Advisor S–O–N–Y–…
Student Er, no, I'll spell it. S–O– N–I–A … then Orr is O–R–R.
Advisor Orr … OK. And you said you were on Hills Road.
Student Yes, but don't send it there as I'm about to move. I'll give you my new address, which is 22 … *Winter Gardens*. That's Glenfield.
Advisor And the postcode?
Student Oh yeah. That's *GF23* …9BQ.
Advisor Fine. Now we're doing a bit of data collection about who uses our services at the moment. Can I just ask a few more questions?
Student Yes, that's fine.
Advisor OK, if you're an international student, what country are you from?
Student I'm from the Netherlands.
Advisor And how old are you?
Student I'm 24.
Advisor And finally, which course are you enrolled on?
Student Right, well that's a bit complicated, since I'm hoping to switch to Economics and History.
Advisor But at the moment …
Student … I'm down to do *Economics and Sociology*. It's a joint degree.
Advisor OK. I'll put that. Great, well … I'll pop the information pack in the post and you should get it soon.

Speaking skills Recognizing similar questions

1
a Students' own answers.
b Students' own answers.
c **Possible answers**
drinking excessive alcohol; infections; not getting enough fresh air; not maintaining good posture; not getting enough sleep

2
b is similar to e
c is similar to j
d is similar to f
h is similar to i

3
a, g   2, 4, 5, 6, 8
b, e   3, 4, 5
c, j   2, 3, 4, 5, 6, 7, 8, 9, 10
d, f   7, 9, 10
h, i   7

111

Emphasizing main points

1

Speaker 1: Questions c or j
Speaker 2: Questions b or e
Speaker 3: Questions h or i

Script

Speaker 1 I think it depends on what interests you and how committed you are. I suppose the best way, or at least the most effective way of getting healthy is through doing more exercise. I mean, diet's important, but you can be thin and unhealthy. So yeah, I'd say exercise is the key thing.

Speaker 2 It's difficult to say, I think. There are so many reasons. The main cause seems to be smoking. I mean, it's the biggest cause of early deaths in most countries, I think. What else? Oh yeah, there's also salt. People eat more than they should do. But actually, people are getting more aware now of the dangers.

Speaker 3 I don't really know for sure, but my impression is that it can help. It's obvious that it helps if you think about it because people keep going back for acupuncture and homeopathy. So, it's mostly because of what people believe. That's what makes it effective.

2

Speaker 3 It's mostly because of …,
Speaker 1 I suppose the best way … is …,
Speaker 2 The main cause seems to be …,
Speaker 1 I'd say … is the key thing.
Speaker 1 I suppose … the most effective way is…,
Speaker 3 It's obvious that …,

Taking time to think

1 b

2

Speaker 1: I think it depends …
Speaker 2: It's difficult to say, I think.
Speaker 3: I don't really know for sure, but my impression is that …

3

Students' own answers.

4

a The first article suggests that exercise might have disadvantages. The second article points out that there may be problems with experts' advice on diet.
b Students' own answers.

5

Students' own answers.

Pronunciation: using two intonation patterns

1

Fall intonation: nine, bee
Fall-rise intonation: diet, question, answer

2

347 fall-rise
347 fall-rise 321 fall

3

a We can show that we have not finished a list by using the **fall-rise** intonation.
b We can show that we have finished a list by using the **fall** intonation.

4

a U
b F
c U
d F
e F
f U
g F

5

Students' own answers.

Exam listening

Questions 11–15

11 Meeting Point: *We are here at the meeting point …*
12 Changing Rooms: *… through the changing rooms …*
13 Sports Hall: *… directly opposite the changing rooms, there's access to our sports hall.*
14 First Aid: *… it doubles as a first aid room in those circumstances.*
15 Café: *… that leads you to the café on one side and the viewing area for the swimming pool on the other.*

Script

Instructor Good morning everybody. I'd like to welcome you to Rose's Health Club which is part of the nationwide Rose Group of Health and Fitness centres. Today I hope to tell you everything about the Glenfield centre and the facilities it offers. First, have a look at the map of the centre I have put up here – there's a copy of it in your information packs. As you can see we have a range of facilities. *We are here at the meeting point* next to the reception desk. If you get lost, which is unlikely, make your way here. The main feature of the health club is, of course, the swimming pool. This is a 25-metre pool divided into three or four lanes. Access to the pool is normally *through the changing rooms*, for obvious reasons. To get to these, bear left as you come through reception and, as you follow the corridor, they are the two doors immediately to your right; first the female changing room, then the men's. If you follow the corridor right to the back of the building you'll find one of our most popular features – three state-of-the-art squash courts with a viewing gallery. We keep them in very good condition, so if you're keen on that sport, I'm sure you'll appreciate the quality. Right then, I'm sure what many of you are thinking of joining for is access to the gym facilities and activities like yoga. We've got lots of space for this, and these are all situated on the left-hand side of the main corridor, opposite the changing rooms and squash courts. At the far end, you'll find the fixed and free weights room – there are lots of fixed weights machines, and you'll also find exercise bikes and rowing machines. Next to that, *directly opposite the changing rooms, there's access to our sports hall*. This is where yoga classes, martial arts, circuit training and other classes take place. We even have badminton and table tennis sometimes. OK, moving on from the sports, there are two other things to point out. One is a small door next to reception, to the left as you come in. This takes you into the staff training room. This is important because you'll know where to find us in an emergency, and *it doubles as a first aid room in those circumstances*. Finally, last but not least, there is another corridor to the right as you come in, and *that leads you to the café on one side and the viewing area for the swimming pool on the other.*

Questions 16–20

16 850
17 250
18 (a) personal trainer
19 during the week/weekdays
20 50

Script

Instructor Now we will go for a little tour in a moment, but first I'd like to tell you a little about the different kinds of club membership we have, so that you can be thinking about what you want as we go round. We first of all have the Anytime membership. Anytime is the complete go-as-you-please membership. This entitles you to full use of all the facilities during all opening hours. And we're open every day from 5 a.m. till midnight. This costs *£850* per year, though there are

Answer Key

some discounts which I will tell you about in a moment. Don't forget that the Rose Group is a nationwide group and this membership also entitles you to the full use of the group's other *250* clubs around the country. The Freetime membership is an off-peak membership. This entitles you to use of the facilities between 10 a.m. and 3 p.m. Also, you can use the facilities at any time at weekends. This costs £500. Note that you will still have access to a *personal trainer* under this membership scheme. Finally, a Standard membership costs £400 and is a weekday membership really, especially suitable for retired people who can come *during the week*. There is also a children's membership scheme. Children can join this scheme if they are between fifteen and eighteen years old. Please note that children under fifteen can't come to the club without an adult and they can't take sessions on the sun bed – not that young people usually want to use a sun bed anyway. The children's schemes are all half-price, that is *50 per cent* for each child or young person in the scheme. People who live outside the area can have a discount of up to 50 per cent, but this has to be arranged specially with the general manager. If that is of interest to any of you, let me know and I will fix up an appointment for you. Now, let's go on our tour.

Unit 10

Topic talk

1
a Students' own answers.
b **Possible answer**
It is perhaps a bit of both. Most individuals can only make small changes within society, which have an impact over time. Some individuals, like scientists and artists, can make huge changes through their work. Society also shapes individuals; otherwise it would be difficult for people to fit in.
c For example, they can help other people who are less able than themselves or less fortunate. They can also aim to make a contribution to society by working hard.

2
b difficulty   f outline
c aspect   g alternative
d area   h attitudes
e issue

3
1 f h
2 g
3 b c d e

4
a proposals
b problem, obstacle, hurdle
c facet
d none
e question
f summary, sketch
g plan
h viewpoints

5
a *theories* replaces *thinking*
b *requirement* replaces *necessity*
c *need* replaces *necessity*
d *topics* replaces *issues*
e *influence* replaces *impact*
f *effect* replaces *impact*
g *concerns* replaces *problems*

6
a international water preservation programme/research into management of assets
b trade and political partnerships/sharing information and technology
c trade and political partnerships/investing strategically in job creation/sharing ideas on how to cope with changes/research into management of assets
d flood prevention/research into management of assets/sharing ideas on how to cope with changes
e sharing ideas on how to cope with changes
f research into management of assets/sharing ideas on how to cope with changes/investing strategically in job creation
g trade and political partnerships/investing strategically in job creation/sharing information and technology/sharing ideas on how to cope with changes

7
Students' own answers.

Listening skills
Paraphrasing questions

1
Students' own answers.

2
Students' own answers.

3
Question 2

4
Possible answers
1 Solomon Asch was born in … .
  The birthplace of Solomon Asch was … .
3 The experiment, which later became so well-known, was called the … .
  Asch's famous experiment was known as the … .
4 The people who took part were mostly … .
  The subjects of the experiment were for the most part … .

5
1 Poland
2 human behaviour
3 line judgement task
4 (effectively) actors

Script
Lecturer In this lecture I want to introduce you to the life and work of a famous psychologist, a psychologist who had a big influence on the field of social psychology. Social psychology deals with group behaviour and the individual as a member of a group, and Solomon Asch made a most important contribution. Solomon Asch worked mostly in the USA, but he was born in 1907 in *Poland*, and he came to the US when he was thirteen. He went to an ordinary high school, and as he had an interest in *human behaviour* he decided to study psychology. He was quite disappointed with his first acquaintance with psychology – it seemed to be all about rats and mice and that didn't interest him at all. However, he persevered and eventually became a professor of psychology. Now, the experiment which made his name is called the *line judgement task*. Participants were asked to compare some simple lines: more precisely, they were given a card with three lines, then were asked to compare another single line and say whether it was longer or shorter than the lines on the card. What a participant didn't know was that in reality, all the other participants were effectively *actors*: that is, they were instructed to give a wrong judgement, and the purpose of the experiment was to see how the single subject would react.

113

Answering visual multiple choice questions

1
Pie chart B.

2
A The pie chart shows that 68 per cent of people gave the wrong answer, whereas 32 per cent gave the right answer.
C The pie chart shows that 32 per cent of people gave the wrong answer, whereas 68 per cent gave the right answer.

3
Possible answers
A There are three vertical lines, side by side, equal distances apart. The shortest line is on the left, the middle-sized line is in the middle and the longest line is on the right.
B The diagram shows three vertical lines of different heights. The tallest is on the left, the shortest is on the right. In the middle is the middle-sized line. They are equal distances apart.
C This illustration shows three lines of different heights, side by side and equal distances apart. The tallest line is in the middle and the shortest is on the left of it. The middle-sized line is on the right.

4
5 C   7, 8   A, E
6 A   9, 10 A, B

Script
Lecturer The subject would hear the others saying things about the length of the line which were clearly false. Most subjects answered correctly in spite of the incorrect judgements of the others, but a proportion – 32 per cent – conformed to the majority view, the incorrect view. This proportion was much, much higher than anticipated. Before the experiments they'd thought fifteen per cent or lower might do this. To give you a bit more detail, I have an illustration up here on the board. A group of six or seven people were given a card with three lines on it. There is a short vertical line, on the right of which is a longer line and on the right of that there is another still longer line. However, it's clear that the longest line is the right-hand one, the second longest the middle one, and the shortest is the one on the left. The participants were given a second card with just one line on it. I should add that in these experiments people became very distressed. They found it very hard to deal with a situation where people were telling them things which were against the evidence of their own eyes. One woman became extremely agitated, running about measuring and looking and checking and shouting in a kind of massive anxiety. Now, experiments which occurred some time later found that other factors can influence the result. For example, when there were more so-called participants, there was even more conformity. On the other hand, when people were able to respond in secrecy, by writing the result down for instance, they made fewer incorrect judgements about the lines. Subjects gave various explanations for why they made the decisions they did. Although they weren't put under pressure by the experimenter, many felt that they would somehow spoil the experiment and upset the person running it if they didn't agree, no matter how stupid they felt. More simply, in other cases they said they just wanted to not show themselves in a bad light. Whatever the reason, Asch's experiment has had a long history and …

Speaking skills Describing places and feelings

1
Text 1: office, workplace, library
Text 2: seaside, beach

2
Students' own answers.

3
a busy   e exciting
b dull   f friendly
c deserted   g peaceful
d wild   h colourful

4
a busy: crowded
b dull: boring
c deserted: empty
d wild: remote
e exciting: vibrant
f friendly: welcoming
g peaceful: quiet
h colourful: sensuous

5
Students' own answers.

6
Students' own answers.

Starting your description

1
Speaker 1: c *fantastic for walking; an amazing atmosphere*
Speaker 2: b *it's mine; I can relax there; gets rid of any stress*
Speaker 3: a *meet my friends; good atmosphere; nice to just sit*

Script
Speaker 1 The place I've decided to talk about is Dartmoor, which is in the south of England. I used to spend a lot of holidays there when I was young. It's a really wild place, fantastic for walking. It's got an amazing atmosphere.
Speaker 2 The place that's really important to me is my garden. It's not very big, but it's mine, and I know I can relax there. Looking after the flowers always gets rid of any stress. And it's colourful too.
Speaker 3 I've chosen to talk about a café I go to in town. It's where I go to meet my friends. There's always a good atmosphere, and it's nice to just sit and watch other people walking past.

2
Speaker 1: The place I've decided to talk about is …
Speaker 2: The place that's really important to me is …
Speaker 3: I've chosen to talk about a … I go to …

3
Students' own answers.

Summing up impressions

1
Possible answers
1 a, b
2 a, b, c, d, e, f, g
3 b, g, h

2
Students' own answers.

Pronunciation: using intonation in continuous speech

1
I was a waiter.	Fall intonation
I worked hard.	Fall intonation
He was a dishwasher.	Fall-rise intonation
The pay was poor.	Fall intonation

2
I worked hard, although the pay was poor.
Part A: fall-rise; Part B: fall

114

Answer Key

3
a 4   d 1
b 6   e 3
c 5   f 2

4 All **Part As** would usually be spoken as fall-rise; all **Part Bs** as fall.

Exam listening

Questions 21–24
21 A … *it's just all a bit of a rush.*
22 C *We're supposed to be comparing the way welfare is approached …*
23 B *… what you write for this is supposed to be unbiased.*
24 A *… 2,000 is the minimum.*

Script
Mike Well, Fiona, we certainly have a lot of work to do this weekend. I wish now I hadn't spent so much time on my other assignment.
Fiona Don't say that! You did really well: 80 per cent.
Mike Yes, but this is different. It's not hard really, *it's just all a bit of a rush*. We had loads of time to get the other one right, but this one is all a bit pressured. That's what makes me anxious, despite the preparation we've done.
Fiona You shouldn't worry. What could go wrong? Come on, let's look through what we can do to make sure it's OK.
Mike Mmm, well, the main difficulty that's bothering me is about defining the terms of reference. It's supposed to be about approaches to social welfare, right?
Fiona Yes, but we're not expected to give a survey of what that means. That's not the point. *We're supposed to be comparing the way welfare is approached* in collectivist societies and what you might call capitalist societies.
Mike So we can concentrate on just that contrast?
Fiona Yes.
Mike The other thing that bothers me is that I'm not really committed to either view.
Fiona Well, I have strong opinions of my own, but that's not supposed to colour my judgement.
Mike How do you mean?
Fiona Well, *what you write for this is supposed to be unbiased. It* specifically says that you shouldn't give a personal view.
Mike But Professor Green has a personal view.
Fiona Yes, but that doesn't mean that we have to agree with him, and I don't think we'll do any better if we do.
Mike Oh. And how long does it have to be?
Fiona The maximum is 4,000 words.
Mike What?
Fiona But that's the maximum. We'll probably end up with about three, but *2,000 is the minimum*. Shouldn't be a problem.
Mike Mm. OK.

Questions 25 and 26
25 the Welfare State
26 Tuesday(s)

Questions 27–30
27 Welfare Economics
28 Mike Green
29 Growing old
30 2013

Script
Mike Now, where can we get some information on all this?
Fiona Well, we could ask Olive over there. Olive, you did this assignment last year, didn't you?
Olive Not this one exactly, but something similar. The most important thing is to get Professor Green's lectures on *the Welfare State.*
Mike Is he good?
Olive Oh, very good. Didn't you know he was lecturing?
Fiona No, no idea.
Olive Well, he is. He's at the Becket Building on *Tuesdays*. I think he's starting this week, so you'll be able to get the series of six. He deals with the underlying philosophy as well as the economics of it all. It's at 10 a.m. – I'd go myself except that I have too much to do.
Mike And what about reading? I've got the reading list here. As usual, it has far more titles and references than we can possibly read in the time.
Fiona I haven't even got a reading list. Where did you get that from, Mike?
Mike I got it at the welcome lecture.
Fiona Oh. I wish I'd gone to that now.
Olive What you need above all is his own book, called *Welfare Economics*. All the department know it and follow his approach.
Mike Oh, right, good idea. Perhaps we don't need to go to the lecture if we have his book?
Olive No, I really do advise you to go to his lectures as well.
Fiona OK, what was the full title of his book?
Olive If I remember rightly, it's called simply *Welfare Economics*, by *Mike Green*.
Mike Oh, I've got it. *Welfare Economics*, Glenfield University Press, 2012.
Fiona Great. Let me just write that down.
Mike Anything else you recommend?
Olive There's Edward Jones's book, erm, *Growing Old* in Britain. That's essential reading but you have to be careful, because it's a popular book by a journalist.
Fiona Well, if it's popular, maybe we'll like it. Who publishes that?
Mike Er. Oh. That's published by Polybus Publications in *2013*.
Fiona Well, that's very useful. I think it's Professor Green for us next.
Mike Right.

115

MACMILLAN EXAMS

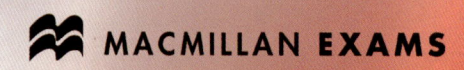

Written by leading IELTS author Sam McCarter, Direct to IELTS provides a short and concise course that combines print and online materials for a more interactive learning experience

- Bands 6.0 – 7.0
- Eight topic-based units cover the skills required for the academic module of the IELTS exam plus grammar and vocabulary build-up
- A 'Writing Bank' provides detailed and focused practice including all task types found in the writing exam and annotated model answers
- The website includes four computer-based practice tests, written by an experienced exam writer, as well as downloadable worksheets to accompany the Student's Book

WITH FOUR **ONLINE** PRACTICE TESTS

DIRECT TO IELTS

Student's Book

Sam McCarter

MACMILLAN EDUCATION

www.directtoielts.com

The IELTS Skills Apps

Exam practice exercises and interactive tasks to help you develop the skills you will need to excel in IELTS.

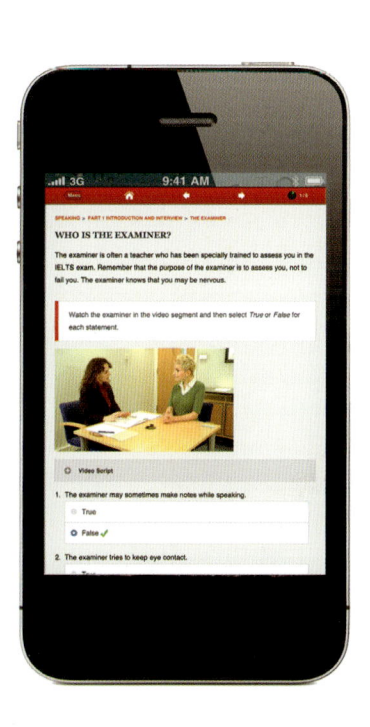

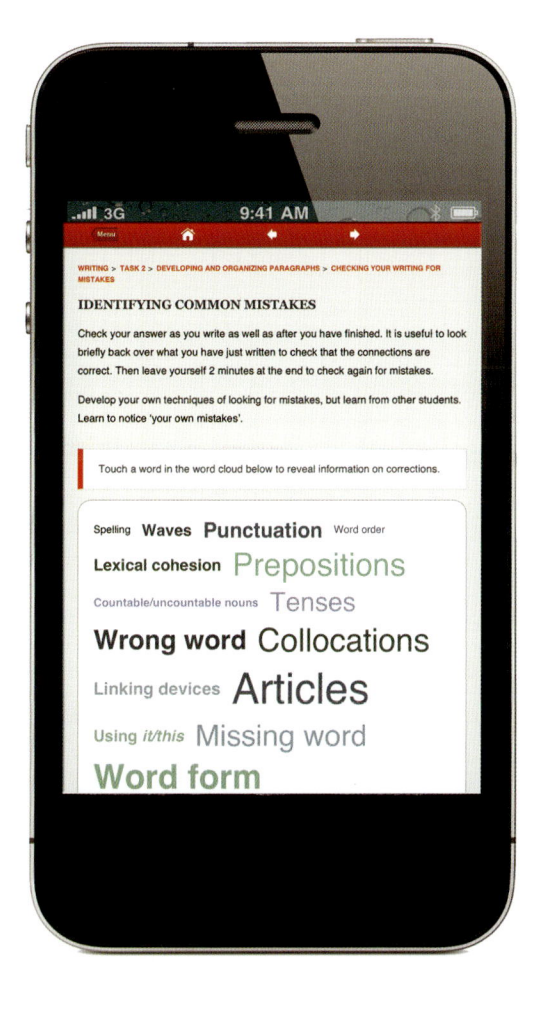

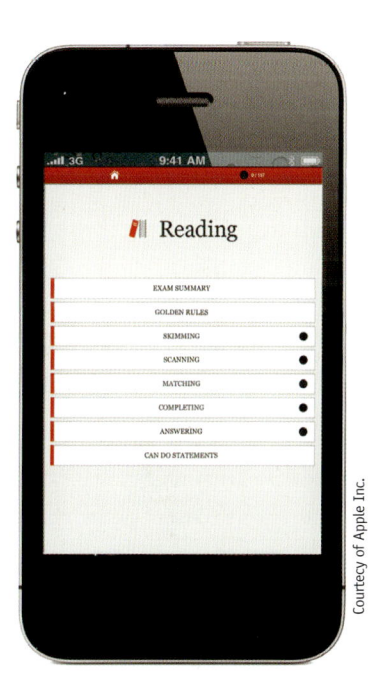

- Written by Sam McCarter, the author of the bestselling *Ready for IELTS* and *Tips for IELTS*
- Each skill is explained and comes with examples and an interactive exercise
- Practise answering the full range of question types that you can expect to find in the IELTS exam
- A detailed overview of the IELTS exam
- Score yourself on the interactive 'Can Do' statement section
- A wide range of innovative and interactive exercises that help you work on the essential skills needed for the IELTS exam

Learn more at the Macmillan Education Apps website: www.macmillaneducationapps.com